# THE WHITE MOUNTAIN
# Ride Guide

**By Marty Basch**

Published by Top of the World Communications
Intervale, New Hampshire

**The White Mountain Ride Guide**
By Marty Basch

**Published by:**
Top of the World Communications
PO Box 731, Intervale, NH 03845

Library of Congress Catalog Card Number: 98-060319
ISBN: 0-9646510-2-5

Book design by Peg DegliAngeli/Snow Pond
Front cover photo courtesy of New Hampshire
Office of Travel and Tourism Development
Inside photos by Marty Basch
Back cover photo by Kevin Murphy

*To Mom and Dad,*
*Thanks for the ride.*

## ACKNOWLEDGMENTS

Many miles went into this book. Thanks go to several people for their help on and off the roads and trails. Thanks to Peter Minnich of Mountain Cycle Guide Service, Steve and Sally Swenson, Mike Miccuci, the people employed by the White Mountain National Forest and New Hampshire Fish and Game Department who furnished me with information, Paul and Peg DegliAngeli, Bobbie Box, Trevor Hamilton, Jan and Jena Duprey, Deni DuFault, Rick Luksza, Ben Wilcox, Alice Pearce, Joel Bourassa, Carisa Flood, Steve, Brian and Donna Finch, John Rankin, Maurice Bransdorfer, White Mountain Wheel People and Anne Kennard.

## ABOUT THE AUTHOR

Marty Basch is a writer whose articles have appeared in various newspapers and magazines across the United States and Canada. He has won several journalism awards for his reporting, and is the author of three books. He has this thing about bikes and boards. Basch lives somewhere in the White Mountains of New Hampshire.

**ALSO BY MARTY BASCH**

Against the Wind
Above the Circle

# RIDE LOCATIONS

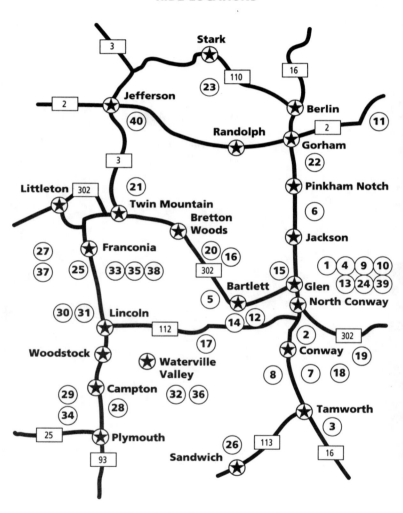

Maps in book are not to scale.

# TABLE OF CONTENTS

## MOUNT WASHINGTON VALLEY

# THE WHITE MOUNTAIN
# Ride Guide

## INTRODUCTION

The White Mountains come alive from the seat of a bicycle. Seemingly endless possibilities exist for the rider, whether it be along a logging road on a mountain bike or a country backroad on a road bike. There are countless miles to explore on forest roads, logging roads, singletrack, doubletrack, snowmobile corridors, trails, abandoned railroad lines, bike paths, bike lanes, backroads and byways.

Along the way, watch for wildlife in the form of deer, moose and even bear. Cycle past streams, snow-capped mountains, waterfalls and still ponds. After the ride, chow down at a White Mountain eatery.

Each season brings new challenges. Mud and high water welcome mountain bikers in spring. Blow-downs from winter's wrath need to be removed. Early road riders might have to contend with roads still dusted with snow or sand and certain mountain roads still closed because the snow hasn't left.

Summer comes and the riding is easy. The roads and trails are corridors for adventure. Come autumn, the colors of foliage steal the show. The mornings have a slight chill, but the days are ideal for riding. Then winter settles in and most riders hang their bikes up for hibernation. But some still ride the roads on cold sunny days after the plows have come while mountain bikers take advantage of frozen, packed snowmobile trails.

The White Mountains have a long history of catering to the outdoor recreationalist ever since Darby Field's first recorded ascent of Mount Washington in 1643. Settlement took off after the French and Indian War of 1763, and soon enough the valleys were being farmed. Word spread of the area's beauty, and by the mid 1800's, farmers were becoming innkeepers. The railroads and grand hotels followed. People came to the White Mountains to play.

Also, the White Mountains provided timber for logging. Abandoned railroad lines are now trails and forest roads.

Many of these rides take place within the 770,000 acres of the White Mountain National Forest in New Hampshire and Maine. The region is rich in hiking trails. Just remember, the future of mountain bike use depends on you. Courtesy is expected. Not every hiking trail is suitable for mountain biking and riding on popular hiking trails is not encouraged.

Mountain biking is not allowed in the five wilderness areas within the forest. They are the Pemigewasset, Presidential Range-Dry River, Sandwich Range, Great Gulf and Caribou-Speckled Mountain. Wilderness areas do not allow motorized vehicles either and are there to preserve and protect. Respect that. Mountain biking is not allowed on the portions of the Appalachian Trail which cut through the area. At times, the Forest Service will post signs to close mountain biking along heavily used pedestrian corridors or areas that have been eroded due to overuse.

Campgrounds, picnic grounds and rest areas are available to both road and mountain bike riders. They offer the opportunity to rest, sleep, eat and refill the water bottles. Several ranger stations and information centers are scattered throughout the region, providing the latest on trail conditions and weather. They are an invaluable resource.

In 1997, the White Mountain National Forest became part of a three-year pilot program which charges a user or parking fee for recreationalists who park at the trailheads and other areas. A sign indicates if the spot is a fee area. A pass costs $5 per week or $20 for the year which runs from May 1 to April 30. The passes are available at the ranger stations, information centers and other facilities.

So choose your trip and ride on!

## ABOUT THIS BOOK

Each of the rides in this book comes with a few pointers at the beginning. The name of the ride, location, difficulty, surface, distance, starting point, directions and food suggestions are included.

How do you rate a ride? Some days are easier than others. The wind blowing in the wrong direction can make any ride a challenge. For the most part, easy rides are those that have relatively flat and gentle terrain. Intermediate rides are more difficult, offering more variations in terrain, like hills, and the distance is longer. Advanced rides are those that are the most difficult and tend to be more technical in terms of handling skills. The climbs are more strenuous, the descents more hairy and some tend to be more remote. They also tend to be longer than those which are more difficult.

Cyclists in the White Mountains will encounter a number of surfaces. For road riders, the surface is basically pavement, though on a handful of the trips a small section of the ride will be on packed dirt.

Mountain bikers have more choices from gravel to the hard-packed forest service roads. Singletrack is a sensation like powder is to skiers and snowboarders. It is a thin path through the woods. Doubletrack is two parallel pieces of singletrack or two well-defined lanes along a forest road.

Distances in this book are approximate as odometers vary, though very little sometimes.

By all means, jazz up the experience out there by taking pieces of suggested rides and turning them into something else.

For example, combine the Sugar Hill Loop and Wells Road Loop into a figure-eight road adventure. Just ride Sandwich Notch Road out and back for a challenging few hours. One thriller is a point-to-point ride from the Kancamagus Highway to Route 302 in Bartlett via the Sawyer River Trail and Sawyer River Road.

Have fun!

## SAFETY

Whether you are riding on the roads or on the trails, being safe will help you enjoy your ride even more. The New Hampshire Highway Safety Agency says most bicyclist deaths result from a bicycle-motor vehicle collision. Head injuries are the most serious injury type to cyclists as well.

So when you head out, make sure you plan your trip by taking a map and keeping an eye out on the weather. Be sure you listen to a weather forecast before heading out. White Mountain weather can change in an instant. Be sure to carry enough food, water and tools before going on a ride. Inspect your bike's brakes, gears, cables and tire pressure before taking off.

Wear a helmet. There are plenty of road and trail demons out there looking to throw you from the saddle. Wear comfortable footwear and riding gloves. Remote areas are no places to ride alone.

Remember, hunters also use the woods in late October and November. Should you head into the woods, wear blaze orange. Better yet, stick to the road during hunting season. During hunting season, there is no hunting on Sundays in Maine. Consider taking one of the rides based in Maine this book relates.

The best off-road riding is usually found between June 15 and Columbus Day weekend. Early season trails and even some roads can still be snow or mud-covered. Blow-downs from severe storms can be hazards. Spring means the rivers, brooks and streams are flowing. During high water, never cross a waterway! If you aren't sure, don't do it.

Fall foliage brings in the tourists. The leaf-peepers tend to start coming in late September and hang around through mid-October. The White Mountains can become congested during this time. If you are riding on the road, be alert.

When it comes to riding the White Mountain roadways, remember that bicyclists are subject to the same traffic laws that apply to motorists. Stop signs apply to you. Cyclists ride with the traffic and not against it. Riders who ride two abreast might consider this nugget from the state's laws: "Persons riding bicycles two or more abreast shall not impede the normal and reasonable flow of traffic, and on a laned road shall ride within a single lane."

The White Mountains have many railroad crossings. Crossing the tracks at high speeds or after a rain can lead to a crash or blowout. Use caution and always cross perpendicular to the tracks.

International Mountain Bicycling Association has set up a list of rules that mountain bikers should follow. Please respect these rules as they are what many mountain bikers live by.

- Ride on open trails only. Respect trail and road closures (ask if not sure), avoid possible trespass on private land, obtain permits and authorizations as may be required. Federal and State wilderness areas are closed to cycling.

- Leave no trace. Be sensitive to the dirt beneath you. Even on open trails, you should not ride under conditions where you will leave evidence of your passing, such as on certain soils shortly after a rain. Observe the different types of soils and trail construction; practice low-impact cycling. This also means staying on the trail and not creating any new ones. Be sure to pack out at least as much as you pack in.

- Control your bicycle! Inattention for even a second can cause problems. Obey all speed laws.

- Always yield the trail. Make known your approach well in advance. A friendly greeting (or a bell) is con-

siderate and works well; don't startle others. Show
your respect when passing others by slowing to a
walk or even stopping. Anticipate that other trail
users may be around corners or in blind spots.

- Never spook animals. All animals are startled by an
  unannounced approach, a sudden movement, or a
  loud noise. This can be dangerous for you, for others, and for the animals. Give animals extra room
  and time to adjust to you. In passing, use special care
  and follow the directions of the horseback riders (ask
  if uncertain). Running cattle and disturbing wild animals is a serious offense. Leave gates as you found
  them, or as marked.

There are a few other tips I would like to pass along:

- Beware of the shade. When cycling along tree-shaded
  areas, look ahead even more while riding. The shade
  can play tricks and make changes in terrain, potholes
  and rocks more difficult to spot.

- Tie your shoe laces. There is nothing worse than that
  invisible hand clawing at your footwear as unkempt
  laces get caught in the pedal.

- Keep your tongue in your mouth while riding. A
  hanging tongue and one bump is a recipe for pain.

Ride smart.

## WHAT TO BRING

What tools do I need? That's a question cyclists frequently ask
themselves before heading out on the roads and trails. It does-
n't matter if you are an ace bike technician or use a tool as a
doorstop, the point is you must carry something to guard
against disaster. Basically, the idea is to get you back home.
Though there may not be a definitive list of what to carry, I have

a few suggestions. Just to give you an idea of some of the things I've carried, at one point during my cycling adventures I carried a miniature bottle of Drambuie and a quarter. I figured if I had to use a tool, I'd need a drink and if I had a drink the tools would be of no use to me so I'd use the coin to make a call for someone to come get me. Also, for those of you not terribly mechanically inclined, my advice is to at least carry the tools and then find someone who knows what to do with them.

If you are just heading out for a day or so, consider taking the following items with you: pump, patch kit, tube, tire levers, Allen wrench set, Phillips head screwdriver, adjustable wrench, chain tool, lubricant, bandanna, Swiss Army knife, duct tape and first aid kit.

If you are planning a short overnight excursion, you might want to take along a few more items: spoke wrench, spare spokes, spare cables and spare chain links.

Not only must a cyclist take care of their machines, but also they must make sure their body is properly fueled. Before taking off on any ride, make sure your water bottles are topped off. Those riders heading deep into the woods where tap water is not available should consider taking either a water filter system or purification tablets in case they misjudge their water intake capacity.

Food is something no rider should be without. Take an energy bar or candy bar at all times. Trail mix and fruit are bicycle friendly. Just watch how you pack those bananas. They can turn to mush.

It's also a good idea to have some food packed in the car awaiting your return.

## BIKEPACKING AND TOURING

Seeing the White Mountains by bicycle can be enhanced by using your rig on a two or three day bicycle tour or bikepacking adventure. Riders can spend the nights by camping out in a tent, shelter or in a hotel, motel, inn, hostel or bed and breakfast.

Whatever your choice, there are a few items you will need to carry with you.

Aside from carrying the tools already discussed, overnight adventurers should have a rear rack on their bicycles. The rack is the mule's tool to carry all those goodies. Personal preference will dictate the type of rack and its placement. Riders can put everything on the rear, or put the saddlebags on the front and sleeping gear on the back.

Though panniers are my preference, riders also use the backpack approach. They either ride with a backpack on their back (not something I recommend) or they affix their backpack to the rear rack with bungie cords and straps.

That's up to you.

What you'll need: panniers (front and/or back), handlebar bag, tent, sleeping bag and sleeping pad.

As to what to take with you in terms of clothing, well, everyone is different. Let's assume this is a long weekend adventure. Depending on your comfort level and season, consider the following: two pairs cycling shorts, riding shirt (perhaps polypropylene), riding tights, socks, rain gear/windbreaker, swim suit, underwear, long pants, warm pullover and running shoes or sports sandals.

Now, helmets and riding gloves are essential. Your map and things you need readily available like baseball cap, sunscreen, mosquito repellent will go in the handlebar bag. Plastic bags are a good idea as they can be used when the rains come.

For those riders who will camp, take along a small stove, fuel bottle, mess kit and lighters. A flashlight, spare waterproof matches or lighter and a candle lantern are good items to have.

Toiletries are up to you. Underarm deodorant is essential. Depending on the length of your trip, consider trial sizes of shampoos. A soap dish which doesn't accumulate soap scum or breaks at corners will make your life easier. Weight conscious riders can use a washcloth instead of a towel.

Take a camera and film. In a notebook, record your adventures. Spare bungie cords are a good idea. Don't forget books, cards or music.

## ANIMALS

Moose, deer, black bear, squirrels and chipmunks are among the many animals which inhabit the White Mountains. You may see them from the seat of a bicycle.

Not all of these sightings have been deep in the woods. Some happen during road rides. Black bears like the garbage dumpsters outside many restaurants, condo complexes and campgrounds. Moose frequent the swampy areas by the side of the road.

The Kancamagus Highway and northern reaches of the White Mountain National Forest are known for their moose sightings. Moose are mostly active at night, but they are spotted frequently at dusk and dawn. Breeding or rutting season is from mid-September through October. Calves are usually born in May or June. So, the best advice offered is to keep your distance should you come upon a moose. Admire it from a distance and then ride on.

Black bears are by nature shy and secretive. They rarely attack or defend themselves against humans. But, they have developed a taste for the garbage people tend to leave around their campsites or dumpsters.

Now, what should you do if you have a close encounter of the black bear kind? The New Hampshire Fish and Game Department offers a few suggestions. Normal trail noise should alert bears to your presence and keep them away. But, if you see a bear, keep your distance. Then, make some noise like talking, clapping or singing. This should make the bear go away. If the bear doesn't leave, it might be attracted to the aroma of food that might be emanating from your bags. Now, black bears sometimes "bluff charge" when cornered or threatened. Stand your ground and slowly back away. Like the moose, admire a black bear from a distance and then ride on.

Should you ever stumble across any type of moose calf or black bear cub, assume that mom is around too and don't go near the kid!

The White Mountains are also home to birds of prey. Every once in a while a cyclist might inadvertently ride near a nesting site. These birds can be aggressive and launch into a dive bombing offense. Best bet is to just leave the area — quickly.

Oh, there are dogs here too. Pedal fast or try spraying them with your water bottle.

## EVENTS, GROUP RIDES AND RACES

Cycling is a social sport. It's great to go out with your friends to explore new roads and trails, but there's nothing like a local to show you the way. Let's face it, stashes of singletrack are closely guarded secrets in these parts. Road riders want to find that backroad that isn't on the state map.

One of the best ways to see the White Mountains is to go on a group ride. The key here is the word "ride." A group ride is not a race. Many bicycle shops in the region set aside a day or so a week where cyclists get together to ride. There's a leader and a different ride is showcased each week. They are free and open to riders of all abilities. Since the times and meeting places sometimes change from year to year, it's best to just ask at your favorite bike shop or pick up one of the several free newspapers in the area to find out where and when they are happening.

Events are another popular way to see the White Mountains. Three riding events immediately spring to the surface. Perhaps the oldest cycling event in the White Mountains is the annual Mud Bath in Plymouth. Normally held in early April, the ride is 17 miles of mountain biking mud and fun. There's mud. There's snow. There's a barbecue too. Best bet is to call the Greasey Wheel in Plymouth at 536-3655.

The White Mountain Fat Tire Festival is another growing event. It's usually held during fall foliage for a few days and encompasses long rides with zany events like a bike toss. To find out more, call the Red Jersey Cyclery in Glen at 383-4660.

One of the finest mountain biking events is the annual fundraiser for the Children's Health Center in North Conway. Called the Trek for Tots, each year riders choose from three loops. They usually range in distance from five to 30 miles. That changes. The ride is held in October. It's one of the area's best kept secrets that won't stay secret much longer. Call the Children's Health Center at 356-5972.

Races rule in the White Mountains too. Bike shops are the ideal resource to learn more about these, and area chambers of commerce usually have them listed in their various magazines and brochures. Bike clubs sponsor races too. Some races are strictly for cyclists, while triathlons have sprung up to include riding. The most visible race is probably the annual Mount Washington Hillclimb. The race to the top of the highest peak in the Northeast is never dull. Great Glen Trails has a twenty-four hour mountain bike race. Several ski areas host NORBA-sanctioned races during the season. There are also weekly citizen races.

# 1. West Side Road and Beyond

**EASY
27 OR 13.5 MILES**

- ■ WHERE IS IT? North Conway

- ■ SURFACE: Paved backroad, bike lane

- ■ DISTANCE: Approximately 27 miles for a loop or about 13.5 miles for an out and back trip with the West Side Road bike lane.

- ■ STARTING POINT: First Bridge Conservation Area, North Conway.

- ■ DIRECTIONS: From North Conway, travel on River Road about .4 miles west of the intersection with Main Street and Pine St.

- ■ FOOD AND STUFF: North Conway Village has bike shops and food shops.

North Conway's West Side Road is a pleasure unto itself. With a bike lane finished in the autumn of 1997, this easy country road is a cycling delight. Just to ride the bike lane and return is a fine outing.

But here, the ride is extended to take in a bit more of the area.

West Side Road is North Conway's most advertised secret in terms of bypassing the traffic on Route 16. It parallels Route 16, meandering past farms with vistas of the Green Hills and Mount Cranmore. Here is an opportunity to have a picnic in an authentic covered bridge spanning the Swift River. Actually, three covered bridges are passed on this loop, plus a state park, towering climbing ledges and a stretch on one of the most scenic roads in the state — the Kancamagus Highway. Farm stands offer the season's harvest. Roll past horses in a field, or stop at a natural food store.

Conway has a few restaurants and shops while a snowshoe museum waits on the Kancamagus. The Albany Covered Bridge is the entranceway to Passaconaway Road which winds its way back to West Side Road.

## 0.0 Start at First Bridge Conservation Area

First Bridge is a popular beach area along the Saco River. Exit the parking area by turning right onto River Road.

River Road heads over another bridge. Hussey's Field, with its awe-inspiring views of Mount Washington, is passed. The red brick building has a tap for water on its side.

## .6 West Side Road (Make left)

Turn left at West Side Road. Admire the views of Cathedral and White Horse Ledges in the distance. Here, climbers challenge the various rock faces. If the ride is taken during berry season, the strawberry stand is worth a stop.

The bike lane starts its 6.2 mile path to Conway. West Side Road is gentle with a few rolling hills. At about 1.1, there is a right which leads to Echo Lake State Park. The mile-long rooty trail along the lake, called the Lake trail, is an easy and scenic mountain bike route.

Pedal by the two restaurants and entryway to a hotel.

Around 3.8, the ride opens up with views of Cranmore, Black Cap and the Green Hills. Working farms dot the road. The road takes a wide bend to the left at about 4.7 and then some railroad tracks are crossed.

The Hickory Natural Foods Store at 5.3 is worth a look while Weston's Farm Stand lay just a half mile ahead.

The Swift River Bridge, built in 1869, is at the 6.7 mile mark. This bridge was slated to be torn down, but a valley-wide effort saved it with private donations. Picnic tables are inside the bridge. Have some lunch. The bike lane ends here.

Many beginners might want to return from here.

Continuing past the Swift River Bridge about .1 mile is an opportunity to view the Saco River Bridge built in 1890. To get there, make a left on East Side Road. Cross the bridge to Davis Park's picnic tables, basketball hoops and tennis courts.

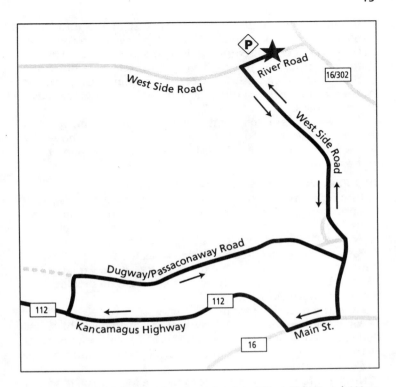

After viewing that bridge, turn back to West Side Road. West Side Road now becomes Washington Street in Conway.

### 7.1 Main Street (Make right)

Turn right at the traffic lights with Main Street (also Routes 16/113). Enter the town of Conway with its movie theatre, gazebo, historical society museum, quick stop food stores and churches. At 7.6 cross the train tracks near the high school.

### 7.9 Kancamagus Highway/Route 112 (Make right)

Turn right at the light for the Kancamagus Highway and ride it for just over 6 miles. The Kanc is a designated Scenic Byway and was opened in 1959.

Shoulder and pavement conditions vary along the Kanc. The

Saco Ranger station, about 100 yards west of the turn, is an excellent information resource. They often have interpretive displays. Water and bathrooms are available. A short spin later, at about 8.1, is Baldy's. You can't miss the totem pole out front. Treffle "Baldy" Balduc, is a bit of a legend in these parts. He makes wooden ash snowshoes. Ask to see the snowshoe museum in the back.

The Kanc passes into Albany as it winds along by the banks of the rocky Swift, climbing and rolling slowly. At 10.6, enter the White Mountain National Forest. Look for the swimming holes in the area.

### 14.3 Passaconaway Road (Make right)

Turn right on Passaconaway Road and head over the Albany Covered Bridge (1858). Toilets are available at the parking area. Cross over the bridge and bear right. This is a good place to relax. The Covered Bridge Camping Area is at 14.8.

Passaconaway Road, also referred to as the Dugway Road, is a bit of a wooded scenic backroad cruiser. It also follows the Swift, with sometimes a birds-eye vista. There is no shoulder, but there isn't much traffic either.

Enjoy the downhill sensation.

Pass a gate during the 15.7 mark, as the section you have just ridden is not maintained in winter. The 17.6 mile mark finds you at the Dugway Picnic Area with its picnic tables, water pump, and steps to the river.

Near the 18.4 mark is a trailhead for the Moats. The road will head through a residential area and sweep around Red Eagle Pond before crossing back into Conway.

### 20.5 Y-junction (Bear right)

Bear right at the junction at the 20.5 mark. You'll soon cross over some railroad tracks.

### 21.0 West Side Road (Make left)

At the stop sign, make a left on West Side Road and enjoy the bike lane once again.

### 26.6 River Road (Make right)

Turn right on River Road and pedal a half mile back to First Bridge to complete this 27.1 mile loop.

# 2. Conway Recreation Trail/ Mineral Spring Loop

**EASY
6 MILES**

- ■ WHERE IS IT? Conway
- ■ SURFACE: Dirt road, pavement
- ■ STARTING POINT: Smith-Eastman Recreation Area on Meeting House Hill Road, just behind the Conway Police Station.
- ■ DIRECTIONS: From Route 302 in Conway, turn on to East Conway Road. The first right is Meeting House Hill Road. Follow it .3 miles until its end.
- ■ FOOD AND STUFF: Bring a picnic lunch. There are also convenience stores along the way.

The Conway Recreation Trail is an ideal adventure for those riders a little unsure of the intricacies of mountain biking. It provides an out-of-the-way experimental playground for families and for those who are new to the sport.

The trail could even be a spot for picnic fun (and swimming once August comes). Along the way, it hugs the banks of the Saco River and provides a glimpse into area history.

The beauty of the trail are signs, placed every quarter mile. They remind riders where they are and how far they have gone along this nearly 3 mile long route. This should allay those fearful of getting lost. The trail, part of Conway's Recreation Trail System, is fairly easy, but in no way flat. There are roots, rocks and sand so beginner riders can get a feel for negotiating various types of terrain.

### 0.0 Start Smith-Eastman Recreation Area
Picnic tables, a toilet, canoe launch and jungle swing are all

poised at the site. The Saco River is in front of you. A posted map is just before the narrow footbridge. This ride goes clockwise. Cross the bridge and the trail gently sneaks up to the left.

Through the trees, the Saco River appears on the left. The trail follows its bank. The large granite abutments in the Saco are what is left of a covered bridge which burned down. Pine needles line the firm path.

At about the .3 mark, the trail descends to a rather sandy section just along the river bank and goes under Route 302. Beware of trolls with literary aspirations who have painted declarations of love and hostility on the rocks.

Round the bend and head up the dirt path, keeping to the left.

### .9 Junction (Make right)

At about the .9 mark, leave the Saco River behind and make a right. There is a sign with an arrow pointing the way. Head into the woods. There will be signs urging caution at times over the next 2 miles. Do not be alarmed. These are for rocks which are easily negotiable, dips which are readily conquered and bridges which are simple to cross.

### 2.0 Mineral Spring

Near the two mile mark, a colorful clearing with wild flowers is entered. Look up off to the left. There, a yellow and green gazebo-type building rests. This is the Mineral Spring in Redstone. The building was constructed in the late 1800's and the site was once home to a bottling plant which provided the soothing waters to the area's grand hotels. But, time and neglect have eroded the building. Look closely at the pool and see the bubbles eminating from the spring.

It is possible to cycle up to the spring. For those cyclists traveling with children, there is an option to cycle the horseshoe-like route by the spring and loop back to the parking area from here along the Conway Recreation Trail.

Continue on and head back into the woods. Stay left and look for the mileage marker which signifies you are continuing on the trail.

Stay straight on the trail through a junction with power lines.

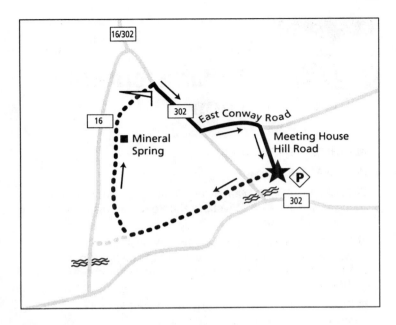

### 3.0 Gate

Close to the 3 mile mark there is a gate and a map. The paved road is Route 302. This is the end of the Conway Recreation Trail. A couple of options exist.

For those who crave fast food, that's just a couple of hundred yards to the left.

If you really enjoyed the Conway Recreation Trail, turn around and follow its length back to the starting point.

A third option is to make a loop utilizing Route 302. A quick right on the pavement will get you on Route 302 for the fastest way back to the Smith-Eastman Recreation Area. Then it's a left on East Conway Road and a right on Meeting House Hill Road.

Whichever route you choose, enjoy.

**ALL LEVELS
23.6 MILES**

# 3. Barnstormers' Loop

- ■ WHERE IS IT? Tamworth

- ■ SURFACE: Backroads

- ■ STARTING POINT: Main Street, Tamworth. Public parking is available on Cleveland Hill Road, across from the Congregational Church.

- ■ DIRECTIONS: From North Conway, travel south on Route 16. Turn right on Route 113 at the light in Chocorua and travel on Route 113 to Main Street in Tamworth.

- ■ FOOD AND STUFF: Tamworth has a couple of general stores. After the ride, try Chequers.

For a new spin on dinner theatre, try the nearly 24 mile long Barnstormers' Loop through Tamworth, Wonalancet and North Sandwich. Of course, cyclists don't have to squeeze in the ride before the 8 p.m. curtain time in summer, nor even go to the show. However, it can be quite an experience.

Sandwiched between the White Mountains and Lakes Region, this bucolic loop offers a moderate ride with some hills along rushing streams, open fields and mountain vistas.

Tamworth is a shining example of Yankee quaintness with two country stores, (including one called The Other Store) inns and a white steeple with clock. The Barnstormers Playhouse was one of the first summer theatres in the country and the oldest in the state. It was founded in 1931 by the late Francis Grover Cleveland, son of the late president. (A Cleveland descendant still haunts the local airwaves).

The route also takes riders along the Chinook Trail, a section

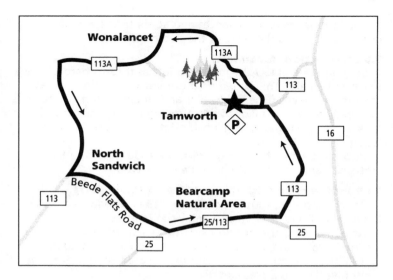

of road named for the famed sled dogs raised in the area which led intrepid explorers to Antarctica. There's a also a chance to visit a covered bridge.

## 0.0 Start at Tamworth, Main Street

The start of this ride is in the heart of New England. Cycle past a church, the Tamworth Inn, Barnstormer's Theatre, two country stores, library, historical society and town offices.

## .3 Intersection with Route 113 A (Make left)

At .3, there is a stop sign. Turn left, heading west on Route 113 A. and enjoy the roller coaster of a ride. At 1.3 miles bear left and stay on the road which now is called the Chinook Trail, in honor of the kennel which bred dogs for Antarctic expeditions. Listen closely for the roar of the Swift River through the pine and birch forests. Cyclists will head against its flow. The road winds through Big Pines Natural Area which is where anglers ply their craft. Stone walls, a cemetery and then Hemenway State Forest await. Hemenway is best explored on cross-country skis and foot, though the trails are okay for mountain biking too.

The road leads to Wonalancet and at about the 5.9 mark, an historical sign tells the story of the sled dogs.

### 7.0 Intersection (Make left)

Stay on Route 113 A by making a left as it turns hard at the seven mile mark. This is one of the finest corners in the state. Take in the view of the fields, hills and steeple. After this turn, get ready for a few miles of more rolling hills. At around 11.2, look for the natural spring on the left if you are in need of water.

Into the land of North Sandwich the road goes, the land of craftsmen and artisans. Homes hide in the woods.

### 13.9 Intersection with Route 113 east (Make left)

At the stop sign, turn left on Route 113 and head east. This is Beede Flats Road. Roll on and enjoy the ramble.

At about 16.2, the option exists for a side trip to a covered bridge. If you want to see it, take a left on Foss Flats Road and cycle about 1.6 miles to the Durgin Covered Bridge over the Swift River. This is a pleasant diversion.

### 17.9 Intersection with Routes 25/113 (Make left)

Turn left on Routes 25/113 and head east. The shoulder returns. There will soon be a convenience store on the left and then one of the smallest post offices around. You might want to stop in to mail a postcard at the South Tamworth office. At about 20.3, look for the Bearcamp Natural Area on the left, a good spot to ponder life's meaning or just hang out.

### 20.8 Intersection with Route 113 (Make left)

Turn left on Route 113, heading east for Tamworth and Wonalancet.

### 21.2 Intersection (Make left)

Stay on Route 113 east, past the general store, by making a left over the Bearcamp River. This is called Tamworth Road.

Soon thereafter, pass an elementary school and Chequers Villa, which has tasty Italian dishes.

### 23.3 Intersection with Main Street (Make left)

Turn left back on Main Street in Tamworth at the 23.3 mark. Cycle about .3 back to the parking area.

# 4. Bear Notch Boogie

**INTERMEDIATE
38.5 MILES**

■ WHERE IS IT? North Conway and Bartlett

■ SURFACE: Pavement

■ STARTING POINT: North Conway Village, parking available on Main Street or near John Fuller Elementary School on Pine Street.

■ FOOD AND STUFF: North Conway and Bartlett have food, water and bike shops.

The Bear Notch Boogie, commonly referred to as the Bear Notch Loop, is a favorite with the White Mountain Wheel People cycling club. It is nearly 40 miles long and offers some glorious scenery along the way. The road surface is good and the terrain varies from level to rolling to one long 5 mile climb up Bear Notch Road.

There are many points of interest along the way like Lower Falls, Rocky Gorge, the Albany Covered Bridge, Attitash Bear Peak ski area and views of the climbing ledges of North Conway.

Possibilities also exist for a short hike to Diana's Baths and a swim in either Echo Lake State Park or in the Saco River by First Bridge once the ride is over.

The ride utilizes many backroads, plus the scenic Kancamagus Highway and bike lane on West Side Road.

### Start 0.0 River Road, North Conway

Where River Road begins, so does this ride. At the intersection of River Road, Pine Street and Main Street (White Mountain Highway), cycle past the traffic light and under the train trestle on River Road. There isn't much of a shoulder on River Road. At

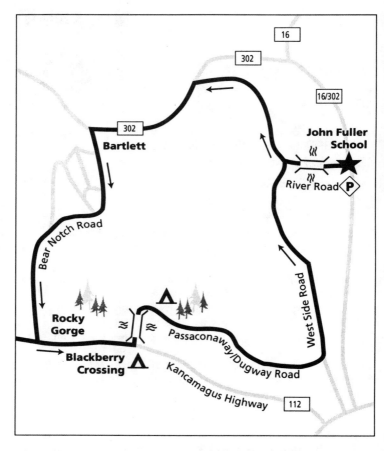

about the .4 mark, you'll pass the First Bridge Recreation Area on the right which is a good swimming spot along the Saco River. Just past it is a brick pump house with a tap spewing fresh, cold water. Look out behind it for Mount Washington views.

### 1.0 West Side Road (Continue straight)

Continue straight as River Road undergoes a name change to West Side Road. You are heading west. Admire the views of

Cathedral and White Horse Ledges. Depending on the season, fresh strawberries wait to be picked at the farm here. At 1.5, there is an opportunity to make a left for Cathedral Ledge and Echo Lake State Park.

West Side Road begins to climb and roll. At about 2.2 on the left is the parking area for the short walk to the pleasant Diana's Baths. Look up at the exposed rock cliffs at about 3 miles and sweep around the curve to the Lady Blanche House. Continue up and at about 3.7, look up on the left and see if you can spot Humphrey's Ledge, a cave.

### 6.7 Intersection with Route 302 (Make left)

Head west on Route 302 by making a left for Bartlett. Route 302 has a narrow shoulder. Try not to be listed on the menu at the restaurant you'll soon see on the right. Soon enough, at about 8 miles, pass by the slopes of the Attitash Bear Peak ski area. Cross the train tracks at 8.8.

### 10.8 Intersection with Bear Notch Road (Make left)

The village of Bartlett has a blinking yellow light. When you see it, make a left on Bear Notch Road. The deli is the last chance for food for some time. After making that left there will be two railroad track crossings coming up. Begin the climb that lasts about 5 miles. Bear Notch Road doesn't have a shoulder.

The first of three scenic pull-outs on the right hand side come into view at 13.3. There are two more before the summit — 14.5 and 15.2.

The road tops out at about 15.5. There will be a scenic vista on the left at the 16.3 as you head down. Chances are you'll be having too much fun to stop.

### 20.0 Intersection with Route 112 (Kancamagus Highway) (Make left)

Near the 20 mile mark, turn left on the Kancamagus Highway and head east. There is a narrow shoulder. Ease on down the road. There are a number of scenic spots to stop and rest. The Kancamagus follows the rocky Swift River.

The entrance to Rocky Gorge appears on the left at 23.2. Take a break to walk over the bridge to Fall Pond.

The Lower Falls Scenic Area at 25.4 is a good spot to watch

the water flow. Walk along the banks. Gaze up at the cliffs.

Both spots are good to have that lunch you brought.

The Blackberry Crossing Campground is passed at 26 miles.

## 26.1 Intersection with Passaconaway Road (Make left)

Turn left on Passaconaway Road. Before crossing over the Albany Covered Bridge, take note that toilets are available. This is also an excellent spot to take some sun on the rocks or cool off in the Swift River. Cross over the bridge and continue on the paved road to the right, soon passing the Covered Bridge Campground on the left at 26.6.

Passaconaway Road is a nice, rolling backroad. It climbs a tad over the banks of the river, but then rolls along it. The Dugway Picnic Area is at 29.4 and has steps leading down to the river.

## 32.2 Intersection with Allen Siding Road (Bear left)

Bear left on Allen Siding Road, cross over the train tracks and bear left again.

## 32.9 Intersection with West Side Road (Make left)

Turn left on West Side Road at the 32.9 mark. You might want to stop in to the Hickory Store for natural refreshment. The bike lane is the chosen path now. The road is one of the best in the White Mountains. See the horses. See the mountains. Ride on.

At about 37.1, there is another opportunity to visit Echo Lake State Park by turning left. There are picnic tables, and a mile long trail around the emerald lake. There are also fine vistas of the ledges.

## 37.5 Intersection with River Road (Make right)

Turn right on River Road. This should look familiar to you by now.

## 38.6 Intersection with Main Street

Find the car.

# 5. Bear, Berry and Brook Loop

**INTERMEDIATE
10 MILES**

- ■ **WHERE IS IT?** Bartlett

- ■ **SURFACE:** Gravel road, singletrack, pavement

- ■ **STARTING POINT:** Parking area along Bear Notch Road.

- ■ **DIRECTIONS:** Head south .9 miles on Bear Notch Road from the light in Bartlett Village. Pass the gate and the parking area is the second right, marked by a brown post.

- ■ **FOOD AND STUFF:** Bike shops are in Glen. Food is in Bartlett Village. There's nothing along the way for water so take everything with you.

Bear Notch has stashes of maze-like rides. This one is fairly simple to follow and utilizes the gravel roads in the Bartlett Experimental Forest, the paved Bear Notch Road itself and some luscious singletrack complete with a stream crossing or two. Okay, there is some climbing here — about 3 miles worth up Haystack Road. However, the reward is ample with a real zinger down Bear Notch and by the time you get back to the starting point, the smile should be such that the steady incline has been forgotten.

Please stick to the roads in the Bartlett Experimental Forest. Renegade bikers have blazed their own trails which does not fare well for the majority of the mountain biking public. The forest is a 2,600 acre outside laboratory formed in a bowl between Haystack and Bear Mountains. There are no signs, but bikers will see numbered lots. Respect the work of those who

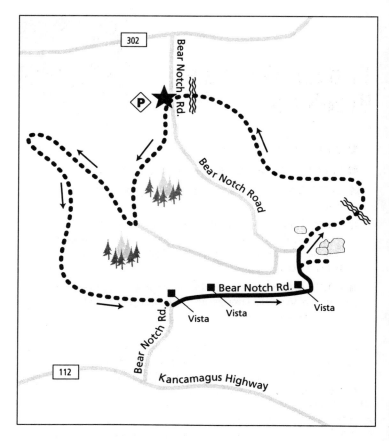

toil in here.

The Experimental Forest is also a slice of berry heaven. Secrets will not be divulged here, but be on the look-out for blackberries.

Just a reminder that vehicular traffic is allowed here. Be on the heads up for a car or two, particularly as you near the top of Haystack Road.

**0.0 Start at parking area on Bear Notch Road**

Begin on the gravel road. Enjoy the winding ride under the cover of the trees. At about .4 a road will enter from the right. Ignore it.

**.7 Junction (Bear left)**

Bear left at the junction at .7. The road rolls up and down here and will soon open up a bit. As a landmark, there will be a clearing at about the 1.5 mile mark and then around the 1.7.

**1.9 Junction (Make right)**

The road comes to a bit of a "T." It is here at the 1.9 mark, turn right. As a landmark, there will soon be a bit of a clearing on the left marked by a couple of boulders. Head downhill and back under the cover of the trees.

**2.7 Junction (Bear left)**

At about 2.7, a triangular island of trees marks a junction. Here, the 3 mile climb begins by bearing left. The road snakes upward. At about 4.2, start to listen for the rushing of the water and try to peer down into the green abyss on the left as you round a hairpin curve. This will give you perspective on the climbing you have done.

After the hairpin, there's a bit of relief, but at about 4.6 start climbing again.

**5.6 Junction with Bear Notch Road (Turn left)**

The return to pavement is the signal you've reached the top of Bear Notch. Turn left here and begin a rip-roaring descent, passing three scenic vantage points. Bear Notch Road is shoulderless. Don't expect to be alone, especially during foliage. Motorists and their passengers will be looking at the views too, so pay attention.

The three vistas, available for your viewing and soul-searching pleasure, come at the 5.9, 6.7 and 7.9 mile marks. All are on the left side of the road.

It helps if you count the three vistas as after passing the third, you will have to find the golden singletrack at an unmarked trailhead.

**8.4 Junction (Turn right)**

Turn right at the unmarked trailhead with two boulders.

Head into the woods on singletrack. Caution: there is a trailhead just before the two boulders that looks terribly inviting. Do not take it.

Smack into the woods, prepare for a steep descent and river crossing. The singletrack that heads into an area with a clearing. At about 8.8, prepare for another steep river crossing.

### 8.8 Junction (Bear left)

After the river crossing, there is a fork in the trail and here you should bear left.

### 9.1 Junction (Bear left)

Another fork, and bear left again. For your bearings, there will be a clearing at about the 9.2 mark and then head straight back into the woods. Caution: at about the 9.4 mile mark, there will be a big rock in the middle of the trail to navigate around. At around the 9.6 mark, the trail parallels Bartlett Brook and the remnants of an old mill are evident.

### 9.7 Junction (Bear left)

At the junction, bear left and cross the brook. After the crossing, bear left for a short, quick spurt up the hill.

### 9.8 Intersection with Bear Notch Road (Turn left)

Turn left on the paved Bear Notch Road.

### 9.9 Intersection with parking area (Turn right)

Make a right into the parking area.

# 6. Doublehead Circuit

**INTERMEDIATE
16 MILES**

- ■ WHERE IS IT? Bartlett and Jackson

- ■ SURFACE: Pavement/gravel road/singletrack/double-track

- ■ STARTING POINT: Parking area at entrance to White Mountain National Forest, off Town Hall Road, Bartlett.

- ■ DIRECTIONS: Town Hall Road is located off Route 16 in the Intervale area of Bartlett. The parking area is about 3.5 miles up Town Hall Road.

- ■ FOOD AND STUFF: This is a somewhat remote ride, and food and water is not available, so stock up.

The Doublehead Circuit through Bartlett and Jackson is a fine two-wheel workout through the woods. The loop, done in the shadows of both North and South Doublehead, is a thrilling mixture of various terrain, including two miles of singletrack on the Bald Land Trail. The descents are marvelous, while the climbing is challenging. It is the technical singletrack that gives the loop an advanced riding flavor.

The ride also takes in two rather steep roads — Dundee Road and Black Mountain Road. Actually, there are six hills of hell (dubbed by a local bike club, the White Mountain Wheel People) on the eastern slope of the White Mountains. They are Hurricane Mountain Road, Thorn Hill Road, Cathedral Ledge Road, Glen Ledge, Blueberry Hill and Dundee Road. Dundee Road is part of this ride, and though it's only a mile climb here, it still can throw sharp jabs to a sleepy rider.

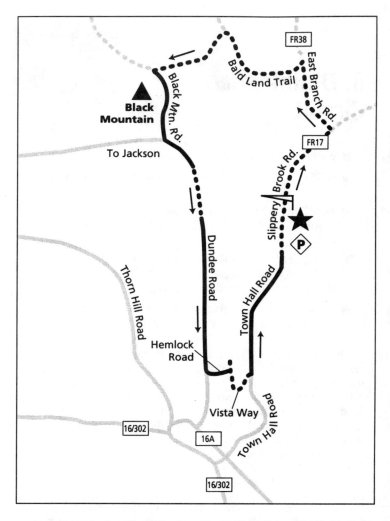

Just a reminder, that the land between the end of the Bald Land Trail and beginning of Black Mountain Road passes through a private section. Respect the land and privacy of the owner.

There are also fine views of Doublehead during the loop.

### 0.0 Start White Mountain National Forest winter turn-around parking area

Leave the parking area on Slippery Brook Road (FR 17) by following the gravel road past both the forest sign and the gate. Slippery Brook Road parallels the Slippery Brook. The road is in good shape and is shaded by trees. The ride begins on a descent, but Slippery Brook will soon ascend for about a mile, passing the East Branch trailhead at about 1.6. It's up and down for another mile.

### 2.6 Junction with East Branch Road (FR 38) (Make left)

Turn left on East Branch Road at about 2.6 and cross over a bridge. Climb for over a mile before the road levels out again, crossing the East Branch via bridge at about 4.6. Soon thereafter, the ride opens up overhead and passes by a swampy area.

### 5.4 Junction Bald Land Trail (Make left)

Turn left at the Bald Land Trail sign and begin the ascent up the singletrack where about a quarter mile later the trail crosses Black Brook Road. Continue straight and follow the sign which points to Jackson and Black Mountain Road. This is a very technical section for about a half mile. Mere mortals might consider taking the bike for a walk, while those who consider themselves deities will ride on.

The Bald Land Trail will soon cross many a ski trail which make up parts of the Jackson Ski Touring Foundation.

### 6.2 Junction with logging road (Make left)

Make a left at the intersection with a logging road, following the sign for the Bald Land Trail.

### 6.3 Junction with scenic vista sign (Make right)

Turn right at the intersection, staying on the Bald Land Trail. Enjoy the descent on the singletrack. At times, the trail will widen and become rocky. There will also be a pair of bridges to cross at 7.1 and 7.3.

### 7.3 Junction with Black Mountain Road (Make left)

Immediately after crossing the bridge, turn left on Black

Mountain Road and leave the White Mountain National Forest. The gravel road heads downward. However, be prepared for a cable gate at about the 7.6 mark spanning across the road. After that, pass by a wooden gate and about 7.8 Black Mountain Road returns to pavement. The road descends steeply.

## 8.4 Junction with Dundee Road (Make left)

Turn left at the stop sign with Dundee Road. A stone cottage and the slopes of Black Mountain are landmarks. Begin an ascent which lasts for just over a mile, taking in views of North and South Doublehead. In about .4 pass the trailhead for the Doublehead ski trail. At about 9.2, Dundee Road reaches the height of land and turns to dirt. Enjoy a zipper of a downhill. Near the 10.5 mark, the road returns to pavement for a steep descent. Before you get too giddy, wait until you see what's around the corner. Don't worry, there's more downhill after that.

## 12.8 Junction with Hemlock Road (Make left)

Hemlock Road is about .4 after Villaggio Bianco. Turn left on Hemlock through a neighborhood of chalets and the road then turns to dirt.

## 13.0 Junction with Vista Way (Make right)

Take the second right on Vista Way, first passing Highland Way. Vista Way has a nice, sweeping downhill.

## 13.4 Junction with Town Hall Road (Make left)

Turn left on the paved Town Hall Road which will lead back to your car. There isn't a sign. The road passes by several residences and will eventually have about a half mile climb starting about the 14.6 mark, and will then change back to dirt at 14.9 where the climb will soon end and the road levels off for the return to the parking area.

## 15.7 White Mountain National Forest winter turn-around parking area

# 7. East Madison Road Loop

**INTERMEDIATE
21 MILES**

- ■ WHERE IS IT? Conway, Madison, Eaton
- ■ SURFACE: Paved backroads
- ■ STARTING POINT: Kennett High School, Main Street, Conway
- ■ DIRECTIONS. Kennett High School is located just north of the Kancamagus Highway on Route 16, which is Main Street in Conway.
- ■ FOOD AND STUFF: There's the general store in Eaton along the way which is worth a stop.

Backroad rambles are a delight. Roll past the tree-shaded cemeteries, pedal by a gleaming white church with its steeple reaching to the sky and relax on the shores of a tranquil lake or at the counter of a general store.

One such loop offers riders various degrees of solitude beginning with the busy streets of Conway, to the see-saw of Route 113 in Madison to the bucolic East Madison Road and then up the enchanted Route 153 in Eaton.

This ride can be done in either direction, but this route follows a counter-clockwise circuit.

### 0.0 Start Kennett High School, Conway

Exit the parking lot by turning right and heading south on Route 16. Cross over the train tracks and ride past the intersection with the Kancamagus Highway. The shoulder will narrow as the road progresses.

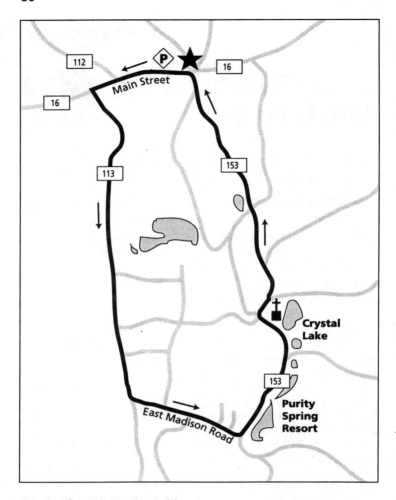

## 1.6 Route 113 (Make left)

Turn left on Route 113 and head west. Because of the businesses along Route 113, cyclists should expect the occasional cement or logging truck. The landscape soon changes from one of scars to a road through the woods. This is rolling terrain.

Snake along past the Carroll County Fish and Gun Glub. At about the 4.3 mile mark, a short diversion can be experienced. The Madison Boulder, a huge geological specimen, is just a 1.4 mile pedal down Boulder Road if you make a right. It's a damn big rock — 87 feet long, 37 feet high and weighing an estimated 24,000 tons.

Back on Route 113, the road rambles on with a nice downhill past an antique store, a bed and breakfast and church.

### 6.4 Junction with East Madison Road (Continue straight)

At about the 6.4 mark, Route 113 turns hard to the right, but you will continue straight on East Madison Road, passing the historical society. The road is not terribly smooth for the first mile and a half, but improves somewhat after that.

Backcountry roads tend to be shoulderless and this holds true of the 4 miles of East Madison Road. Up and down it rolls along fields, stone walls and homes. The last mile is a zip of a downhill past Camp Tohkomeupog and the Stone Environmental School.

### 10.8 Junction with Route 153 (Make left)

Turn left on Route 153, heading north. The meandering Route 153 is the epitomy, without the cliche, of White Mountain quaintness. The King Pine ski area, reflecting lakes, a white church and a village store where a dog can lay at the patrons' feet await. The road snakes upward gradually. At around 14.5, enter Eaton and cycle past the church, cemetery and inn. Stay on Route 153 by taking the hard right. It is in the Eaton Village Store that cyclists can take a break. Or, head .3 to the shores of Crystal Lake and look for the picnic tables among the trees.

Big rollers continue out of Eaton for another 4 miles until things level off outside of Conway village.

### 20.4 Intersection with Route 16 (Make left)

Traffic lights mark the intersection with Route 16. Turn left, and head south, passing through Conway's Main Street with its movie theater, convenience stores and restaurants.

### 20.9 Kennett High School (Make right)

Turn right in the high school parking lot to end the ride.

**EASY
12 MILES**

# 8. Fowler's Mill/ Chocorua Loop

- ■ WHERE IS IT? Tamworth
- ■ SURFACE: Dirt roads/backroads
- ■ STARTING POINT: Fowler's Mill Road (sometimes called Chocorua Lake Road).
- ■ DIRECTIONS: The road is in Tamworth, located off Route 16, 10 miles south of Conway, near Lake Chocorua.
- ■ FOOD AND STUFF: Food and water is not readily available during this ride, though there is an inn which offers lunch.

How many times have you driven up to Mount Washington Valley, looked out of the window at Mount Chocorua and never stopped? Well, you are about to run out of excuses. This loop is the reason. Mount Chocorua is arguably the most photographed peak in all of New Hampshire. Though just under 4,000 feet high, the mountain stands tall in the reflection of itself in the shimmering waters of Chocorua Lake. Throw in winding dirt roads, a wooden bridge, and a shoreline picnic area complete with wood chips, and you have the makings of a delightful backcountry ramble. That's exactly what you will find in a network of dirt and secondary roads in Tamworth, located off Route 16.

This ride passes through the Hemenway State Forest, but most the circuit goes right by private homes. Though you may wish you lived here, please respect the privacy of those who do. Stay to the roads, and do not trespass, no matter what view you see through the trees.

Basically, this is an easy ride. However, easy does not mean flat. Fowler's Mill Road does have a hill to climb. So does Gardner Hill Road.

There are toilets located at the beginning of the ride.

## 0.0 Start Fowler's Mill Road parking area, Tamworth

Leave the parking area on Fowler's Mill Road, head over the bridge and enter a peaceful, tree-covered neighborhood. The dirt Fowler's Mill Road gently rolls a bit, and at the .6 mark, stay to the right at the fork with Loring Road.

## .9 Fork (Bear left)

At about the .9 mark, a second fork is encountered. Stay on Fowler's Mill Road by bearing to the left, looking for the sign that says the road is not maintained during winter. At about 1.8, you will see a road sign for Fowler's Mill Road and Philbrick Neighborhood Road. Stay on Fowler's Mill Road. Enjoy the descent which begins around 2.5. Near the 3.4 mile mark, Paugus Mill Road is passed, and its sign pointing to the Liberty and Brook Trails. Cross over the bridge. At times, the road can be a bit washboard like.

## 4.7 Intersection with Route 113A (Make left)

At the stop sign which marks the intersection with Route 113A, turn left as the road turns to pavement and cross over the bridge.

## 4.8 Intersection with Old Mail Road (Make left)

After the bridge, turn left on Old Mail Road for a return to dirt and head up the hill. In about .4, you will enter the Hemenway State Forest. Old Mail Road rolls along for just over 2 miles.

## 7.1 Intersection with Gardner Hill Road (Make left)

Turn left on Gardner Hill Road for nearly two miles as the road returns to pavement. There is no street sign indicating this is Gardner Hill Road. The road climbs before treating you to a descent.

## 9.0 Intersection with Route 113 (Make left)

A stop sign and church marks the intersection with Route 113.

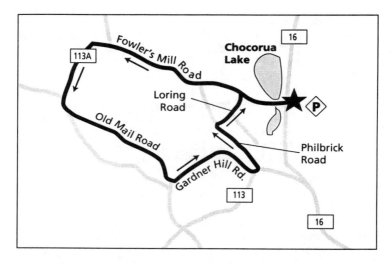

Make a left on the pavement, descend and prepare for another quick turn.

### 9.1 Intersection with Philbrick Neighborhood Road (Make left)

Turn left on Philbrick Neighborhood for a return to dirt. Descend and soon pass the entrance to Staffords in the Field, an inn which sometimes hosts contra dances.

### 10.5 Intersection with Loring Road (Make right)

Turn right on Loring Road. There is no sign. However, there is a small wooden bridge and if you cross over it, you're going the wrong way. Follow Loring Road around, and down.

### 11.3 Intersection with Fowler's Mill Road (Make right)

Loring Road comes to an intersection. Here, turn right on Fowler's Mill Road.

### 11.9 Fowler's Mill Road parking area

Grab that picnic lunch, find a spot under the trees and enjoy the views of Mts. Whiteface, Passaconaway, Paugus and Chocorua.

# 9. Moat Mountain Meander

**ALL LEVELS
8 MILES**

- ■ WHERE IS IT? North Conway
- ■ SURFACE: Forest road, singletrack
- ■ STARTING POINT: Forest road 379 gate, North Conway.
- ■ DIRECTIONS: From North Conway, take River Road one mile and make left on West Side Road. Travel 2.7 miles to Cedar Creek and make right. First dirt road on right follow .4 mile to forest gate. Very limited parking.
- ■ FOOD AND STUFF: Take food, take water as there is nothing along the way.

The Moat Mountain Meander is suited for many different types of riders. The trek is really an out and back stretch to a deadend with views of North, Middle and South Moat Mountains. It is ideal for all levels as the beginning 2 miles or so is relatively flat for beginners, while the 2 mile climb is terrain better riders would want to tackle. The reward is easy. It's down-hill on the way back.

However, this ride has extremely limited parking. In the summer months, it is suggested to make this a much longer journey, actually cycling from North Conway along the bike lane and adding over 5 miles to the roundtrip journey. Just follow the directions above. During the off-season, parking by the gate is a much easier task.

The sensitivity is in the access to the forest road. The road skirts a condo development. Respect the privacy of those who

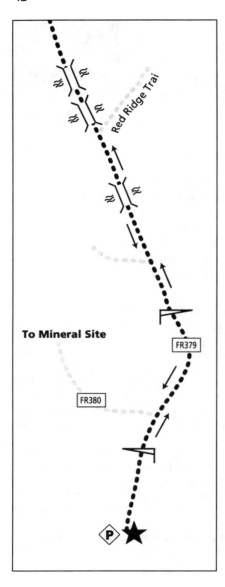

live there and heed the signs requesting no parking on the grass shoulder.

Forest road 379 is a beautiful ride in North Conway. The road is wide enough for two to cycle abreast. The road is smooth too. Near the end, more advanced riders will get a slice of singletrack as the road deadends.

### 0.0 Start Forest road 379 gate

Begin by cycling past the gate on the virtually flat smooth surface. It stays this way for about a mile until the road dips slightly to pass by a swampy area. Depending on the amount of rain, this section can be a bit wet. After passing it, there is a gentle incline. After about 1.6 miles, an unmarked forest road is passed on the left. This is FR 380. Continue straight on FR 379. It will sweep to the left at about the 1.9 mile mark. At the 2.1 mile mark, another forest gate is passed. This is a good turnaround point for the beginner rider, who upon the return to the first gate, will have traveled some 4.2 miles.

FR 379 climbs here. At about 2.2, a trail comes out to the left. This is part of the Moat Mountain Smokey Quartz Loop. Continue the climb up the hill. At about 2.9, you start getting views of the Moat Mountains. The road levels off a bit. Up ahead will be a short rocky section where the road crosses a wash.

On the other side, cross a wooden bridge at about 3.3. The road begins to narrow a bit and soon the singletrack experience will begin. Ignore that arrow that points to the right (That's the demanding Red Ridge Trail). Stay straight.

Two more wooden bridges will be crossed as you ride under the glory of the mountains.

### 4.1 Clearing

The ride deadends in a clearing after 4.1 miles. It ends here because the land beyond it is usually posted.

Turn around and return the same way you came.

**ADVANCED
8 MILES**

# 10. Hurricane Mountain Loop

- ■ WHERE IS IT? North Conway

- ■ SURFACE: Pavement, singletrack, doubletrack, gravel road

- ■ STARTING POINT: Whitaker Woods Conservation Area Parking Lot, Kearsarge Road, North Conway.

- ■ DIRECTIONS: From North Conway Village, turn at the traffic light with Kearsarge Road. Follow Kearsarge Road all the way, as it bears left at the top of the hill. From there, the trailhead is about a mile on the left side of the road.

- ■ FOOD AND STUFF: Cranmore, during the ride, is a stop for water and food. North Conway has bike shops, food and restaurants.

This loop is a killer. When you have cycled its entirety, never placing your foot on the ground, you will ascend to the level of master mountain biker. Hurricane Mountain Road is steep. It is pure, unfiltered pain. One of its pitches contains a grade of 15 percent. The average pitch on the Mount Washington Auto Road is 12 percent. The ride also features the Black Cap Trail, a rooty and rocky trail enjoyed by hikers. The Cranmore Trail has some of the finest, sweetest singletrack around while zipping down Cranmore Mountain Resort is a brake-pumping experience with incredible North Conway views.

Be aware that part of this ride is on private property — Cranmore Mountain Resort. The ski area does allow mountain bikers to pass through the property during this loop. However, you ride at your own risk.

Because there are several options for the Cranmore descent, actual mileage will vary from rider to rider.

### 0.0 Start Whitaker Woods Conservation Area
### parking area

Exit the parking area by turning left on Kearsarge Road. Remember that transfer station and power lines in front of you. Kearsarge Road passes through a residential area with inns and ski clubs.

### 1.1 Junction with Hurricane Mountain Road (Make right)

Turn right at the stop sign at the four corners onto Hurricane Mountain Road. Like Kearsarge Road, Hurricane Mountain Road is shoulderless and passes by homes and ski clubs. It also goes by the trailhead for the Kearsarge North Trail at about 1.5.

### 2.0 Steep, winding road warning

Hurricane Mountain Road, at this point, is not maintained during winter. The pavement, at times, reflects this. Near the 2 mile mark, there is a sign warning of a steep, winding road ahead. Believe it. Hurricane Mountain Road narrows dramatically and enters the woods along Kearsarge Brook. Remember, this is a two-lane road used by vehicles. Start climbing for 1.7 miles. The Black Cap Trail is just before the height of land, but you should pedal up to the crest in the road and see the sign that says 15 percent grade for 2 miles. Mortals rest. Gods continue.

### 3.7 Black Cap Trail (Make right)

Turn right on the Black Cap Trail. Black Cap, with its blazes, will be your path for the next .7 mile. It is rocky, rooty and will ascend. Again, it is popular with hikers heading to its summit. Mountain bikers are not allowed on the summit as it is part of the Green Hills Conservation Area. About a half mile into Black Cap, you'll pass a signboard describing the Green Hills.

### 4.4 Mount Cranmore Trail (Make right)

Turn right by a series of blazes on the Mount Cranmore Trail. Prepare for about 1.2 miles of narrow and technical singletrack that is mostly heading downhill. There is one very steep and

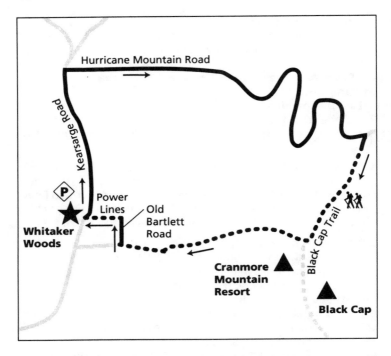

sharp pitch going up, looking like a wall, at about the 5.4 mark. Following that, the singletrack plunges dramatically to the ski area.

### 5.6 Junction with Cranmore Mountain Resort (Make right)

At about the 5.6 mark, the trail intersects with the maintenance road at Cranmore Mountain Resort. The easiest way down is to make a left here and head down the winding gravel road.

Turn right here and pedal up to the summit of Mt. Cranmore, passing the broadcasting towers and then the Dogger Haynes summit patrol shack. There is a restaurant at the summit with a deck.

There are a number of ways down featuring a variety of terrain. Hardcores like the Ledges Trail which leaves from the restaurant while a less challenging way down is via the Kandahar Trail. Options exist during both descents for expert singletrack.

## 5.7 Descend
Head down for the ride, about two miles!

## 7.5 Ski lodge
At about the 7.5 mark, you should find yourself in front of the ski lodge with a statue of Hannes Schneider, the father of modern skiing. Follow the paved ski area road out, passing through the dirt parking area, to Old Bartlett Road.

## 7.6 Old Bartlett Road (Make right)
Turn right at Old Bartlett Road. There is no sign. Ride along past condos.

## 7.8 Power lines (Turn left)
A red fire hydrant on Old Bartlett Road is your cue to turn left on a singletrack right-of-way under power lines back to the place you started. During this final stretch, there are two forks. Both lead to the same place. At each fork, taking a right goes through the brooks, while taking lefts go over bridges. You'll see the transfer station ahead.

## 8.1 Kearsarge Road
Cross Kearsarge Road and head back to the parking lot.

**ALL LEVELS
18.6 MILES**

# 11. Wild River Road

- ■ WHERE IS IT? Evans Notch
- ■ SURFACE: Forest road, logging road
- ■ STARTING POINT: Wild River Road, located in Hastings, Maine off Route 113 in Evans Notch.
- ■ DIRECTIONS: Leave Gorham, head west on Route 2 to Maine. Make a right on Route 113 and travel three miles to trailhead, which is signed.
- ■ FOOD AND STUFF: No food! Water is available along the way. Gorham is the place to fill up.

The Wild River Valley is a gem to explore and the canopied Wild River Road is the path to discovery. Located in Evans Notch, Wild River Road, also called Forest Road 12, follows the river, crosses over three brooks and provides access to three bridges spanning the water. It is the way to both a campground and shelter which might be the enticements for an overnight mountain bike adventure. It is also a good spot for cycling families and those new to the sport. Those who are unsure as to how far they really can cycle always have the opportunity to turn around and head back, downhill, to the car.

The road is fairly level at times but in reality, is a gradual incline with a hill or two. It begins as a fairly easy forest road, turns onto an old logging bed with two stream crossings and eventually crosses the Spider Bridge leading to the Spruce Brook Shelter.

Please note once Wild River Road turns into the Wild River Trail it becomes a popular hiking trail, particularly during sum-

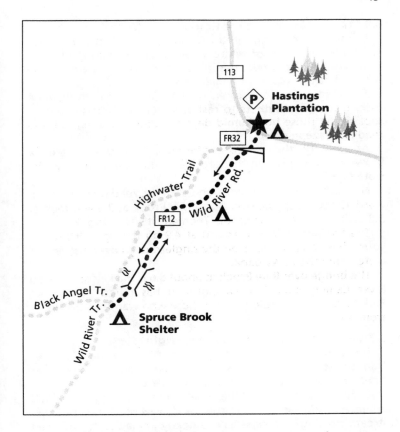

mer weekends and holidays. Use common sense and courtesy along this section.

Water is not available at the onset of the ride, but does become available at the 5.7 mile mark at the green handpump in the Wild River Camping Area. This ride begins in Maine and crosses into New Hampshire.

Before setting out on the ride, check out the suspension Highwater Bridge, a short ride or walk from the parking area.

## 0.0 Start parking area off Route 113

Leave the parking area. A sign tells of the Hastings Plantation, 67 acres of white spruce and red pine planted in 1930. The road continues past a gate and a swampy area to the left at about a quarter of a mile.

The road follows the banks of the Wild River with its large rocks inviting sunbathers to rest and waters inviting bikers to cool off on those hot, humid days of summer. During fall, the road is ablaze in color.

At about 1.5, the road crosses into New Hampshire. There is a brown marking post on the left side of the road indicating the state line.

Near 2.4, there is a .2 climb, and then the road rolls on downward. Cross the bridge over Burnt Mill Brook at 2.8 and then at 3.2 cycle over Dewdrop Brook. Then 4.7, it's Twin Brook.

The Shelburne Trail is crossed at 4.9 on the right. It's worth your while to cycle the .1 on the singletrack to peer out on the water from the rocky bank.

The bridge over Blue Brook at about 5.6 is the key to the Wild River Campground. The campground has toilets and water. Parking is also available here for those who want to start riding from here.

## 5.7 Wild River Campground (Bear right)

The campground — which has water — is some 5.7 miles from the starting point. This is a fine turn-around for beginner riders. The rest of the ride is a bit moderate.

Cycle to the fork, past the toilets, and bear right. The road enters a cul-du-sac and here the trail leaves right. Two rideable stream crossings are experienced nearly immediately, followed by an invitation to sign the trail log. This is the Wild River Trail. The path is an old logging railroad bed. It is a gradual incline. The trail switches between smoothed-over rocks to dirt. Enjoy it.

## 6.0 Junction with Moriah Brook Trail (Stay straight)

Stay straight on the Wild River Trail. It is your path for 2.7 miles. But, if you take a right here, you can take a look at another suspension bridge, the Wild River Bridge. It's well worth it.

The road continues along the south side of the river, passing a clearing and then going on a short section of doubletrack.

After this, the trail narrows at about 6.8 for about .1 on single-track. Less advanced riders should walk here as the trail is on a narrow ridge.

Then it heads back into the woods along the river banks and widens out. At about 7.4, there's another stream crossing.

## 8.4 Intersection with Spider Bridge (Turn right)

Turn right and cross Spider Bridge.

## 8.45 Intersection Highwater Trail and Wild River Trail (Turn left)

Make a left after crossing the bridge and continue on the Wild River Trail. It follows an old railroad grade. At about the 8.5, the Black Angel Trail diverges from the right. It's about .8 to the Spruce Brook Shelter.

## 9.3 Spruce Brook Shelter

Turn around and head back, or stay the night. Those turning around here and heading back to the parking area will have completed an 18.6 mile roundtrip once back at the beginning.

**INTERMEDIATE
14.2 MILES**

# 12. Lower Nanamocomuck

- ■ WHERE IS IT? Near Bartlett
- ■ SURFACE: Singletrack/forest road/pavement
- ■ STARTING POINT: Trailhead with the Lower Nanamocomuck Ski Trail on Bear Notch Road.
- ■ DIRECTIONS: To reach the trail from Bartlett Village, proceed up Bear Notch Road by the blinking yellow light some 8.3 miles. The trailhead is on the right. From the Kancamagus Highway, turn on to Bear Notch Road and proceed about a mile. The trailhead is on the left.
- ■ FOOD AND STUFF: Bring it with you. No food is available, but there is water at a campground.

A ski trail by winter, the Lower Nanamocomuck serves up some of the finest singletrack in the Mount Washington Valley — some 6 miles of it. It follows the banks of the Swift River, offering excellent vantage points for views. But, to reach the cache, cyclists must put up with rocky, technical sections and muddy areas where it is advised to walk bikes.

There are several bridge crossings along this well-signed route, and an opportunity to view the beauty of Falls Pond and the Rocky Gorge Scenic Area off the Kancamagus Highway. Cycling is not allowed by the pond and gorge areas due to their popularity with hikers and walkers. Should you decide to visit, please respect this and be like a pedestrian — walk.

The Albany Covered Bridge is crossed near the end of the Nanamocomuck. There is an area there which has toilets. Carry food and water on this one as it is not available. This area is popular with tourists, particularly on weekends.

Please note that the first .7 miles of this trail is fairly rocky and technical, but certainly passable. This can be avoided by heading .2 miles north from the trailhead on Bear Notch Road to Forest Road 209. Turn right and climb the Forest Road until about .7 when a sign indicates the Paugus Link trail. Turn right and follow it .3 miles until it hooks up with the Lower Nanamocomuck.

## 0.0 Start Lower Nanamocomuck Trailhead

Cross Bear Notch Road and enter the woods by the sign indicating this is the Lower Nanamocomuck Trail. Rocks, roots and bridges wait to embrace you. At about .7, the trail merges with the Paugus Link. Stay to the right and head on down. The trail reaches the Swift River. It winds and rides like a roller coaster. Try not to hurt your face by smiling too much.

At about 1.5, cross over the bridge to an intersection with the Paugus Ski Trail. Just bear to the right. About a quarter mile later, be prepared for a bridge crossing that appears out of nowhere. After the bridge, the trail offers a fine view of the Swift from high on the eroded river bank. More bridges are crossed over the next half mile. The trail rocks and rolls.

## 3.7 Intersection with Wenonah Trail  (Bear left)

Around the 3.7 mark, a bicycle sign points to the left. This is the Wenonah Trail and it is your path. Make the left.

Please note, those wishing for a shorter ride can make the right and walk to the Rocky Gorge Scenic Area, a fine place to contemplate man's existence while having a snack. From there, bang a right on the Kancamagus Highway and ride it to Bear Notch Road by making a right. The trailhead is about a mile up the road. Those continuing on the Wenonah Trail will have the Rocky Gorge opportunity on the ride back.

The Wenonah Trail is also a cross-country ski trail, and climbs steeply for about .4 mile before leveling out and then descending. Prepare for a bridge crossing. There is also a muddy section to conquer.

## 4.7 Intersection with Lower Nanamocomuck (Bear left)

Rejoin the Lower Nanamocomuck Trail by bearing left at the

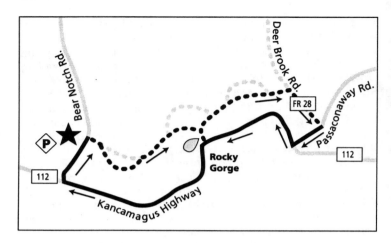

sign. The next mile is muddy and technical. The trail heads back to the Swift. The trail passes the Wenunchus Trail and will soon ease.

### 6.0 Intersection with Deer Brook Road (Make right)

Turn right on Forest Road 28 which is Deer Brook Road. This is a strong descent to the Albany Covered Bridge. The paved road at this point is the Passaconaway Road. Just a short spin up is the Boulder Campground. The area around the bridge is a fine spot to loll about the rocks.

Cycle over the bridge and head for the Kancamagus Highway. Before reaching the "Kanc" there is an area with toilets.

### 7.2 Intersection with Kancamagus Highway (Make right)

The ride back along the Kancamagus to the trailhead passes by many scenic areas well worth making a stop. First, the Blackberry Crossing Campground is passed. Further on, Lower Falls, a popularity sunning and swimming spot is passed. After that, it is Rocky Gorge.

### 13.3 Intersection with Bear Notch Road (Make right)

Turn right on Bear Notch Road and head up about 1 mile.

### 14.2 Lower Nanamocomuck trail

Welcome back!

**INTERMEDIATE+
5 MILES**

# 13. Moat Mountain Smokey Quartz Loop

- ■ WHERE IS IT? North Conway
- ■ SURFACE: Singletrack/Forest road
- ■ STARTING POINT: Moat Mountain Smokey Quartz parking area
- ■ DIRECTIONS:  From North Conway, take River Road one mile to West Side and turn left. Follow West Side some 5.5 miles to Passaconaway Road and turn right. Travel 1.2 miles to High Street, an unmarked road bearing right (which has a mineral collecting sign nearby). Drive High Street and it will become FR 380. Proceed and bear left at the gate.
- ■ FOOD AND STUFF: No food or water is available. North Conway and Conway have food and restaurants.

The Moat Mountain Smokey Quartz Loop is a bit like a credit card. In the beginning there is the thrill of instant, total satisfaction. But after the gratification, it's payback time. There are those riders who may find paying back to be a small task. However, there are those who may find the 1.2 mile climb known as payback to be long, arduous and demanding.

The nearly five mile loop gets its name from the Moat Mountain Smokey Quartz Area the rider skirts. The area is a spot in the White Mountain National Forest where hobbyists collect minerals. Cyclists will see some of the huge boulders. Because of the site, be courteous should you come upon walkers heading out to the site.

The ride begins on some singletrack that is a tad rocky. There are two stream bed crossings along the way. However, the beauty of this ride is the views off to North Conway, taking in the climbing ledges, Kearsarge and the Green Hills. After the gnarly descent, the loop continues on gentle forest roads. The long climb will be on a forest road which levels off and dips back to the parking area.

## 0.0  Start at parking area for Moat Mountain Smokey Quartz Mineral Site.

Though there is no sign, the Mineral Site Trail begins through the huge boulders. Cycle through them and head into a clearing. Up ahead — near the .1 mark — you will come to a fork where an arrow on a brown sign points to the right. Bear right and follow in the direction of the arrow. Into the woods you go. The trail is marked by orange blazes and is a tad rocky at the onset. The rocks are readily negotiable by intermediate riders. At about .4 the first of two stream beds is crossed. About .1 later, another one is crossed. This section is steep and though rideable, caution should be used. At about the .7 mark, there is an intersection with a huge boulder. Just continue straight here.

Near the mile mark a sign welcomes you to the mineral collecting site. Stay straight on the trail. Just after the mile mark, the trail takes a swift bend to the right and begins a long, scintillating descent, complete with rolling bumps through a clearing. The clearing is reached about 1.4. Enjoy the views of the Mount Washington Valley before heading back into the woods.

## 1.6 Intersection with FR 379 (Make right)

At about 1.6, turn right and continue down the hill on FR 379. It is unsigned, but at about the 1.75 mark, you will come upon a gate. Continue past it, enjoy the descent and sweep around the corner.

## 2.2 Fork with FR 380 (Bear right)

Near the 2.2 mark, there is a fork where riders bear right on FR 380. This road is unsigned at this junction, but in about .2 you'll be crossing a one-lane wooden bridge. The nicely-packed road rolls at this point.

Roll on. At about 3.3 the long winding climb begins.

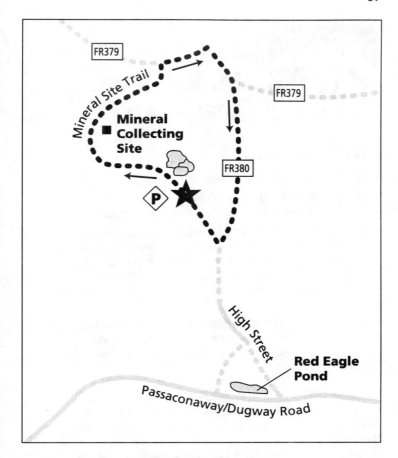

### 4.0 Intersection with FR 379 (Make right)

Take a breather at the gate. Then turn right on FR 379 and climb about a half mile more before the road levels off. After it does, there is a short dip back down to the car.

### 4.8 Parking area for Moat Mountain Smokey Quartz Mineral Site.

Hope you enjoyed the ride!

**EASY
12.3 MILES**

# 14. Rob Brook Road Loop

- ■ WHERE IS IT? Bartlett

- ■ SURFACE: Logging road/pavement

- ■ STARTING POINT: Trailhead with the Lower Nanamocomuck Ski Trail on Bear Notch Road.

- ■ DIRECTIONS: To reach the trail from Bartlett Village, proceed up Bear Notch Road by the blinking yellow light some 8.3 miles. The trailhead is on the right. From the Kancamagus Highway, turn on to Bear Notch Road and proceed .7. The trailhead is on the left.

- ■ FOOD AND STUFF: Bartlett and Glen have restaurants and bike shops. Water can be found at the various campsites along the way, but stock up on food before doing this one.

Looking for a relatively easy adventure? This is it. Rob Brook Road is a meandering and rolling forest road. Remember, the White Mountain National Forest is a live and working forest. The road winds by streams and huge boulders, but there are also signs of harvesting. A few quick climbs are rewarded with refreshing downhills. To the rider new to mountain biking, this ride offers a chance to take things somewhat easily. Rob Brook Road is wide enough to cycle two abreast on a good gravel surface. The road is well-marked. Near the end of the road, there is an opportunity to ride singletrack and cross the Swift River. Plus, the ride heads on to the scenic Kancamagus Highway with a chance to stop and learn a little about the area's history while strolling through a graveyard and homestead.

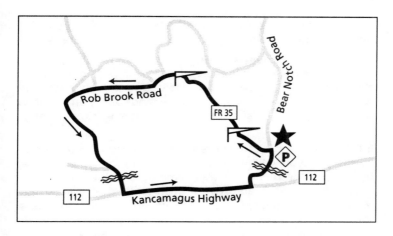

### Start 0.0 Trailhead with Lower Nanamocomuck Ski Trail, Bear Notch Road

Rob Brook Road is a gated road also known as Forest Road 35. Leave the trailhead by going around the gate and proceed along the road through the woods. Along the way there will be several crossings with other trails like the Lower Nanamocomuck, Brunel and even one called Rob Brook Trail. Stay on Rob Brook Road the entire way. Wooden signs will point the way. There are several sweeping turns during this roller of a ride, and in some stretches, keep on eye out for vistas of distant cliffs.

### 2.8 Gate (go straight)

The gate is usually open. Continue on through it and stay on the gravel road. The road will level out a bit, but soon the road will be like riding a multi-humped camel.

Some of the landmarks coming up will be an old gravel pit and a sweeping curve to the left by a bog. It might be a good place to dip your feet in on a hot summer day.

### 8.3 Junction (go straight)

Stay on Rob Brook Road. That means go straight. As a landmark, on your left you will see a sign for the Nanamocomuck trail. Past it will be a huge boulder. The terrain changes from gravel to a jeep-like lane with high grass. This gives the trail a singletrack-like essence. Enjoy the few hundred yards of it because soon you will be staring into the waters of the Swift.

### 8.6 Swift River (river crossing)
The rushing waters are those of the Swift. During low water, the river crossing is easily negotiable. During high water, just forget about it. Cross the water to the sandy banks on the other side and follow the trail to the right, on the singletrack through the high bush.

### 8.8 Junction with the Kancamagus Highway (make left)
It is likely you will hear the cars on the Kancamagus Highway before you see them. The trail comes out to the edge of the paved road. Quickly adjust your attitude from off-road to on-road so you can deal with the vehicles. Make a left and ride on the narrow shoulder.

### 9.6 Campground
The Kancamagus is a nice, gentle ride. The Passaconaway Campground will appear on the left while the parking area for the Downes Brook Trail will be on the right. Keep on eye out for moose in this section. A couple of wet, boggy areas by the road-side are prime feeding grounds.Pass by the Olivarian trailhead too which is on the right.

### 11.2 Historic Site
Step back in time at the Passaconaway Historic Site, with its gravesite and Russell-Colbath House on the left. Soon thereafter is the Jigger Johnson Campground on the left.

### 11.6 Bear Notch Road (make left)
Turn left on Bear Notch Road for the last leg of the ride. It is about .7 back to the trailhead on the left hand side of the road. The good news is that the first half of that is gentle and crosses an area with inviting sandy beaches. The bad news is that last half is uphill.

But, when you get back to the trailhead, you now know where to go for a swim.

### 12.3 The end
Trailhead with Lower Nanamocomuck Ski Trail, Bear Notch Road.

# 15. Rocky Branch Loop

**EASY
7.3 MILES**

- ■ WHERE IS IT? Glen
- ■ SURFACE: Forest road, pavement
- ■ STARTING POINT: Parking lot for Patches Market on Route 302 in Glen, located .3 west of the lights at the junction of Routes 16 and 302. Two bike shops in the area, Boardertown and Red Jersey Cyclery, located just west of the intersection, allow parking too.
- ■ FOOD AND STUFF: Patches has what you need for sustenance. Top off the water bottles.

The Rocky Branch River is aptly named. Its huge boulders create clandestine swimming holes and invite riders to take a snooze in the summer sun. This is a short, funky ride which allows bikers to ride on both of its shores, cross it and take in a bit of the eclectic residences which are found in its vicinity.

Though small in terms of distance, the Rocky Branch Loop is big on fun. The ride begins on a rolling backroad which turns to dirt and then heads into the White Mountain National Forest. There is a taste of single rack, a river crossing and a gentle downhill.

### 0.0 Start parking lot
Ride west by taking a left out of the lot on Route 302 and pedal the shoulder. See the distant slopes of Attitash and ride parallel to the train tracks of the Conway Scenic Railroad.

### .7 Intersection of Jericho Road (Make right)
Turn right and head north on Jericho Road, a shoulderless

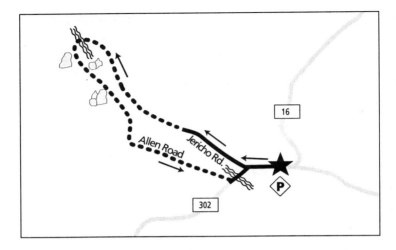

backcountry road. The road will be the path for 2.5 miles, and winds through an area of homes ranging from log cabins to mobile homes. After about 1 mile, there is a half mile pull up hill before Jericho Road turns to dirt.

The road descends after that. At about the 2.8 mile mark, the road heads into a small neighborhood of camps. Be sure to look for the "hiking boot tree" on the right side.

### 3.2 Unmarked parking area (Make left)

Turn left near the 3.2 mile mark by an unmarked parking area. Enter into the trailhead and head through those two huge boulders. The trail is a nice section of singletrack which follows the waters of the Rocky Branch. Be sure to take in the views as you pedal along near its banks on the ridge.

### 3.5 Cairn (Make left)

Okay, this is the funky part of the ride. It's time to cross the river and head to the other side. The easiest way to get to the other side is making a left at a cairn (pile of stacked rocks) near the 3.5 mile mark. There is usually a ribbon tied on a tree here too. Do not cross the river during times of high water!

Now, should you miss this turn, do not panic. In a few hundred yards the singletrack will peter out by a gravel road. Here, you can bushwhack, carefully, to the other side of the river, pick up the trail on the other side and follow it downstream. Should you cross here, you'll know how the river got its' name. This is not a smooth bottom river. It is not an easy task.

So, at the cairn, make that left and pedal down to the river bank. Across the river, you should see a dilapidated cabin to the right and another residence high on the left. Cross the river here.

### 3.8 Allen Road (Make left)

Head up the sandy shores and make a left. This is Allen Road. The well-defined dirt road changes from dirt to roots to sand to rocks, but it is a gradual downhill and an enjoyable spin along the river bank.

### 5.1 Swimming hole

Since this is one of those rides where it's difficult to keep your shoes dry, you might as well get everything wet. Near the 5.1 mile mark on the left side of the road is a clearing with a sign that forbids camping there. Enter the clearing and find the path to the right. Follow it down a couple of hundred feet and come to another clearing. Look down to the river at that swimming hole and those huge slabs.

At about the 6.0 mile mark on Allen Road, the road returns to pavement.

### 6.2 Junction with Route 302 (Make left)

Allen Road ends at an intersection with Route 302. Make a left and ride on the wide shoulder.

### 7.3 Parking lot (End)

There's the parking lot. Go eat something.

**INTERMEDIATE
12.5 MILES**

# 16. Sawyer River Road/Carrigain Brook Road Loop

- ■ WHERE IS IT? Hart's Location
- ■ SURFACE: Logging road/doubletrack/ singletrack/river crossings
- ■ STARTING POINT: Sawyer River Road trailhead, Hart's Location.
- ■ DIRECTIONS: The trailhead is 4 miles west of Bartlett Village (the blinking yellow light) on Route 302.
- ■ FOOD AND STUFF: Bring it with you. Bartlett Village has a deli and a couple of restaurants.

The gravel Sawyer River Road (FR 34) and the doubletrack Carrigain Brook Road (FR 86) team up for a beautiful ride along the upper Sawyer River. Sawyer River Road is a vital link between the Kancamagus Highway and Route 302. During this ride, sweeping views of 4,680 Mt. Carrigain can be spotted with its ranger tower up top. The road also passes through the now defunct logging town of Livermore which was thriving in the 1800's. The ride does head out into moose country and provides for ample berry when in season.

Though the ride does begin on a steady 4 mile incline, the return makes the trip worth it as the road winds down along the rushing Sawyer River. Another plus is the change of terrain. From river crossings to singletrack, there is enough diversity to keep the loop interesting.

Sawyer River Road, with its secret swimming holes and access to the Sawyer Pond Trail, does see a fair amount of use by vehicles.

### 0.0 Start Sawyer River Road Trailhead

Just start up Sawyer River Road or leave the parking lot by riding on the Sawyer Pond Trail for about .3 mile. This old railroad spur bypasses an early section of the Sawyer River Road.

### .2 Junction (Make right)

Turn right at the junction, following the arrow.

### .3 Junction with Sawyer River Road (Make left)

Turn left on the gravel Sawyer River Road and begin the climb above the river. At about 1.5 miles, there are signs of the old Livermore logging community like stone walls and abandoned buildings. A gate here leads to a cottage with a picnic table and river access.

The road is a steady grade, but there is some relief on the way. At about 2.1, the Signal Ridge Trail and parking area is reached.

At about 3.9, the parking area for the Sawyer Pond Trail is reached. There is also a gate and a footbridge spanning the river. This is a good spot to rest before heading on.

### 4.0 Fork with Carrigain Brook Road (FR 86) (Bear right)

Bear right at the fork on Carrigain Brook Road. The road turns to doubletrack, with some sandy and rough spots, along a 2 mile stretch before a bridge crossing. After being under a canopy of trees, the road opens up a bit, first by a boggy area, then with views of Mt. Carrigain and followed by a sand pit.

After about a half mile, the road starts to roll downward and flattens out a touch, snaking through the woods. At about 5.4, a rough, washed-out rocky section must be navigated for about .3. Stick to a side for the best ride.

### 6.1 Bridge Crossing (Bear left)

The road bears to the left at about the 6.1 mile mark and crosses over a bridge. Head over, and enter the woods for some singletrack. About 200 feet later, stick to the left as a shadow of an old trail gives the appearance of a fork.

### 6.3 Junction (Make left)

The singletrack then comes to a T-junction over a washed-out logging bed with large rocks. Turn left here on Carrigain Brook Road. There is singletrack here too that is technical with its

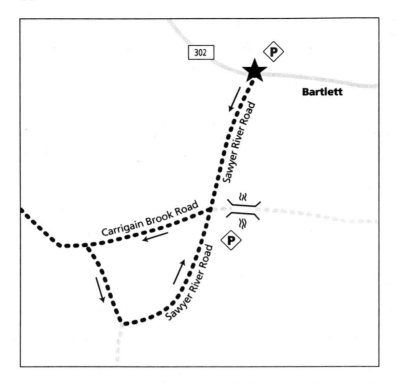

roots, rocks and wet sections. It might be best to walk the rough spots.

### 6.5 River crossing

Cross over the Sawyer River if conditions are safe. The trail widens out a bit here and zips down for about .3 mile alongside the river. Be prepared for a small section or two with rocky, but rideable patches.

### 6.9 Stream crossing

Cross another stream.

At about the 7 mile mark the road comes into a clearing. Follow the logging road by bearing left.

## 7.2 Intersection with Hancock Notch Trail

Stay straight on Sawyer River Road at the intersection with the Hancock Notch Trail. The road smooths out here on the gravel road and winds up a bit. At 7.6, stop at the clearing on the left. That's Mount Carrigain with the ranger tower in the distance. It is said the summit of Mt. Carrigain offers some of the finest views in all of the White Mountains. To the left of the tower is a rock face called "The Captain." At 7.7 the road starts to wind down on doubletrack. The Sawyer River Trail is passed at 8.3 and a bridge is crossed soon thereafter, but you'll probably be going too fast to notice. At around 8.5 you'll be in familiar territory again with gate and footbridge over Sawyer River.

Roll on back down for just under 4 miles. Remember, shadows can play strange tricks on the terrain. Pay attention to the road ahead during this fun descent.

## 12.1 Right at arrow

Turn right at the arrow to ride back on to the trailhead from where you started.

## 12.2 Left at arrow

Turn left at the next arrow.

## 12.4 Back at trailhead parking lot.

**INTERMEDIATE+**
**15.3 MILES**

# 17. Sawyer River Trail/Sawyer Pond Trail Loop

- ■ WHERE IS IT? Near Albany, off the Kancamagus Highway

- ■ SURFACE: Hiking trail/forest road/singletrack/pavement

- ■ STARTING POINT: Sawyer River Trail parking area.

- ■ DIRECTIONS: The small parking area is about 3 miles west of the Sabbaday Falls picnic area on the Kancamagus Highway (Route 112).

- ■ FOOD AND STUFF: Bring everything you need! If coming from Conway, stop there for food. If Lincoln, that's the last food stop.

Unspoiled Sawyer Pond is one of the gems found during this treasure of a ride. The real reward though is the singletrack scattered throughout a jaunt that encompasses hardpack, bridges, river crossings, rocks, roots and mud. Though both the Sawyer River Trail and Sawyer River Road section of the ride are relatively easy, it is the rocky, rooted Sawyer Pond Trail and its exhilarating singletrack which puts this route closer to the advanced level.

Bikepackers take note. There are platform tent sites and a shelter at Sawyer Pond which could break this ride down into an overnight. The camping is primitive. Bring your own drinking water.

## 0.0 Start Sawyer River Trailhead

Let gravity work and descend along the Sawyer River Trail,

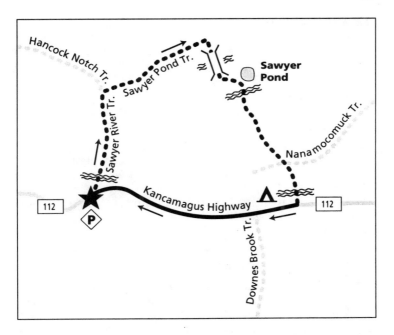

over exposed rock, and come smack to the banks of the river after only about a .1 spin. The trail bears right and it's another .1 to the chilly waters of the Sawyer River.

### .2 River Crossing

During stretches of high water times, its is advisable not to attempt to cross the river. For the most part, it is passable.

The Sawyer River Trail follows an old railroad bed on the other side of the river. The grade is somewhat easy.

### .6 Junction (Stay straight)

The Nanamocomuck Ski Trail is on the right and slips down the bank, but stay straight. The trail starts a gradual climb up the west bank of Meadow Brook and crosses a wooden bridge at about .7 mile. This is the beginning of several bridge crossings. The current of the brook flows against the rider. Look for beaver dams along its flow.

### 1.3 More bridges

Take a look at the surrounding peaks while crossing a bridge with railings. The trail continues through open bog areas which are places moose like to call home. Wooden planks have been placed in certain sections to help cyclists navigate the mud.

### 2.3 Bridge sign

Maybe this section should be called "Bridge Alley." Nearly half a dozen lay in the trail's path.

### 2.6 Junction (Right)

The trail comes out on to a "Y" area. Make a right on to the well-defined dirt road, Sawyer River Road (FR 34). (Left is the Hancock Notch Trail). The road snakes along. There is a gradual climb, dip and then it flattens out for a bit. At about 3.4 miles there is winding downhill.

### 3.7 Bridge

The stunning river crossing via bridge calls out for a photo opportunity if you can stop.

### 3.9 Junction with Sawyer Pond Trail (Make right)

The narrow footbridge is the landmark one must cross to hook up with the Sawyer Pond Trail. Before crossing the bridge, sign the register. The Sawyer Pond Trail is a restricted use area which means no camping along the trail.

Cross the footbridge. The trail bangs a left, heads up some step-like stones and continues hard right. This section is very rocky and rooty for over a mile. At 4.2, cross another wooden bridge and smoothes out somewhat for about .2.

### 4.4 Large Boulder

Some riders at this point might feel a bit like that huge boulder on the left side of the trail. A tree has wrapped its octopus-like roots around it and appears to be squeezing — hard. Don't fail to take note of the rushing stream on the right side of the trail. There are also water bars and culverts along the trail. The trail ascends for about a half mile.

### 5.2 Sign

The sign says you are entering a forest protection area and the trail shortly heads to the left.

### 5.3 Junction (Make right)

Sign points to the Sawyer Pond Trail. Warnings indicate that black bears might like to pass on through. Should you be camping, store your food accordingly. Make a right. The trail is rooted and narrow.

### 5.5 Junction (Make right)

Sawyer Pond sits before you. Here, tent platforms, a shelter and toilet can be found to the left. There are a number of spots just on the banks which invite rest, sustenance, conversation and libation. Perhaps the cry of a loon will break the silence.

Cross the river. From here, it's about 4.5 miles of thrills. Begin by carefully negotiating your way across the rushing water. After a couple of hundred feet of rocks and roots, the single-track begins. Smile.

Descend through the technical terrain.

### 6.3 Big Rock

The trail takes a hard right and quick dip around a rock that wants to reach out to snag you. Just be alert. Look out for the water bars. At about the 7 mile mark, the trail becomes snake-like. There's a steep section or two. The yellow blazes are reminders of what trail you are on.

### 7.3 Junction (go straight)

The Sawyer Pond Trail crosses with a snowmobile trail. Continue straight. There is a gradual incline for about .3. Then the roller coaster points downward for about a half mile.

### 8.3 Junction (go straight)

The Sawyer Pond Trail intersects with a gravel logging road. The intersection is rather sudden after that downhill. Continue straight.

The roller coaster continues for about .3. There could be a little muck.

### 8.9 Junction (go straight)

To the left is the Brunel Trail. Stay on the Sawyer Pond Trail.

### 9.3 Junction (go straight)

To the right is the Nanamocomuck Trail. Stay on the Sawyer Pond Trail.

### 9.8 Junction (go straight)

To the left is the Nanamocomuck Trail. Stay on the Sawyer Pond Trail. The singletrack becomes narrower and vegetation tries to grow over it. Boom! It comes out on the banks of the Swift River.

### 9.9 River Crossing

At times of high water, the Swift River is dangerous to cross. Use caution.

### 10.0 Parking lot

The trailhead is here for the Sawyer Pond Trail. Cycle about .1 to the Kancamagus Highway and make a right back onto the paved road. The Kancamagus has a narrow shoulder during the ride back to the start of this loop. The first couple of mile of the ride back is relatively easy.

### 10.8 Camping

On the left is the Downes Brook Trailhead and on the right is the Passaconaway camping area.

### 12.0 Picnic Area

On the left side of the road is the Sabbaday Falls Picnic Area. It's a short walk to a small waterfall. The winding Kancamagus starts to climb at about the 13.6 mile mark. The road will not relent until you stop at the Sawyer River Trail parking area. There is a brief respite at 14.1 miles in the Sugar Hill Overlook will you can see some of the terrain you have just conquered.

### 15.3 Finish

The Sawyer River Trail parking area completes the loop.

**MODERATE
24 MILES**

# 18. Snowville Loop

- ■ WHERE IS IT? Conway, Eaton and Brownfield
- ■ SURFACE: Paved backroads
- ■ STARTING POINT: Main Street, Conway. Parking is available on Main Street.
- ■ FOOD AND STUFF: Conway has plenty of stores and restaurants.

Yes Virginia, there is a Snowville and on this rambling back-road loop through two states, along farms, barns, by orchards and shaded woods, you will pass right through it. This rolling ride on the eastern flank of Mount Washington Valley is a show-case of what life can be like for those who choose to slow down a bit.

Shoulders are mostly a memory on this one. But the majority of the ride from Conway to Eaton, through Brownfield, Maine and back to Conway doesn't have much traffic.

### Start 0.0 Main Street, Conway.

Leave Conway and head south by the traffic light on Route 153 to Eaton. Route 153 rolls about 5 miles to the shores of Crystal Lake in Eaton. There are picnic tables, a white-steeple church in the background, Foss Mountain in the foreground and should you need it, the Eaton General Store is just a few hundred feet up Route 153 from here.

### 5.2 Intersection with Brownfield Road (Make left)

Turn left on Brownfield toward Snowville. There is a sign which points the way to Snowville and Brownfield, Maine. Like

153, this one rolls too, with a couple of sharp hills along the way. About a mile later, pass by Snowville with its cluster of neat, white homes by the roadside. The Snowvillage Inn, built in 1916, is located just off a side road here. Brownfield Road meanders by the side of a stream for a spell, and is shaded by trees. At about the 8 mile mark, look for "Frog Rock" on the left side of the road. It is not exactly the area's Blarney Stone, but those looking for a prince might want to kiss, or at least rub, the rock to see if anything materializes. If it does, please drop us a note.

Near 9 miles, there is a boggy area near the road which looks like a nice spot for a moose party. At the 10 mile mark, welcome to Maine. There is a sign.

At about 10.4, prepare for a thriller down "Asparagus Hill." The hill takes its name from the farm, which has a sign reading "asparagus" during the spring.

## 12.5 Intersection with Brownfield Road (Make left)

Turn left on Brownfield Road. There is no sign indicating the name of the road, but there is a sign pointing to North Conway, NH and that's the way you want to go.

The Brownfield Road is hilly, and starts off on a gradual 3 mile incline. Along the way, you will pass old stone walls, farms and orchards.

Following the climb is a short descent and then another short, steep uphill.

At the top is the state line for New Hampshire at about 15.2. Valley road riders use it as a finish line during a sprint. Other less-athletic riders might use it as a place to rest.

At about 19.3, the road passes by Conway Lake with its town beach. There is a toilet here, and a short, quarter mile walking path to the old Henry Cotton Mill. From the beach, Brownfield Road is now named Mill Street. It will soon pass a school and head into a residential area.

## 20.1 Intersection with East Main Street (Make left)

Turn left on East Main Street. A shoulder returns. This is Center Conway. Frye's Store is an ideal stop to re-fuel, particularly if you like pizza. There are pay telephones there too, and right next door are the Conway Town Hall. This is Route 302/113.

At about 21.5, there is a blinking yellow light. Stay straight on

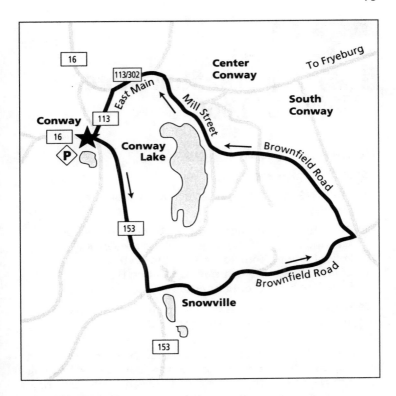

Route 113 West.

One more half mile hill awaits at about the 22 mile mark, but then it's down back to the starting point.

### 23.7 Intersection with Route 153 (Go straight)

Pass the traffic light and you're back on Main Street in Conway Village. Find the car.

**INTERMEDIATE 35 MILES**

# 19. Stow Store Loop

- ■ WHERE IS IT? Conway

- ■ SURFACE: Pavement

- ■ STARTING POINT: Smith Eastman Recreation Area, Conway

- ■ DIRECTIONS: The Smith-Eastman Recreation Area on Meeting House Hill Road, just behind the Conway Police Station. From Route 302, turn on to East Conway Road. The first right is Meeting House Hill Road. Follow it .3 until its end.

- ■ FOOD AND STUFF: The destination is a store. There are convenience stores along the way.

Some of the most pleasant backcountry roads in Mount Washington Valley are found among the farms and rolling hills near Conway. Here, the roads dart between Maine and New Hampshire. The atmosphere is rural and the scenery changes from fields to mountain vistas.

One of the finest refueling stops for cyclists is the Stow Corner Store in Stow, Maine. Its' pastry will revive. Its' little ice cream cones have got to be one of the biggest small cones in the world, at least we think so. Its' beer and wine selection is eclectic for such a location. Quite often, cyclists will make the pilgrimmage just to ride back stocked with freshly baked breads and bear claws. The delight too is relaxing on the deck outside the store. Yes, the store goes for a mall in these parts.

The beauty of this ride is that it has some of the flattest roads in the area. There are a few rolling hills, but nothing terribly demanding. Combine food, friends and meandering backroads

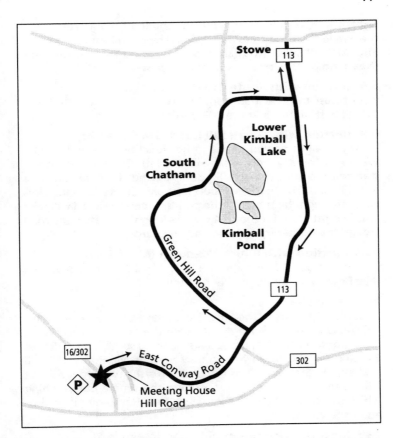

and make this a fun outing, no matter what the season.

## 0.0 Start Smith Eastman Recreation Site, Conway

Leave the parking area, cycling up Meeting House Hill Road to the stop sign.

## .3 East Conway Road (Make right)

Turn right at the stop sign, .3 into the ride, on to East Conway Road and go over the train tracks. There is a narrow shoulder on this flat to rolling country road. At 1.6, there is a market on the right. The road rolls along with the shade of many trees. Near the 5 mile mark the trees are replaced by open farms with views into Maine's hills. Two farms offering roadside refreshments (Nearfield and Sherman) will soon be passed.

### 5.9 Junction with Route 113 (Stay straight)
Just past the Sherman stand, there is a junction with Route 113. Stay straight on Route 113 north.

### 6.9 Junction with Green Hill Road (Stay straight)
Stay straight as you pass another junction with Route 113. Webster's Country Store will be on the left. Green Hill Road will start to have some rolling hills soon. Pass the Chatham town line at 10.3 miles. The road meanders past old cemeteries and offers views through the trees of little ponds. Green Hill Road will take a hard right at about the 14.4 mark. Along this stretch, the road crosses the border into Maine and Fryeburg.

### 15.8 Junction with Route 113 north (Make Left)
Turn left at 15.8 onto Route 113 and head north. Less then a mile later, cross the town line for Stow.

### 18.7 Stow Store
Route 113 leads to the Stow Store. Have fun. Stock up. Relax a little. Once done, leave the store on the same road you came on — Route 113. This time, you are heading south. Follow Route 113 and see the world from a new perspective. Route 113 will snake a bit. Stay with it as it passes a North Fryeburg school at 22.1 with bucolic farm views. Admire the simple but stunning white church up ahead built in 1838. New Hampshire is re-visited at the 28.4 mark.

### 28.5 Junction with Green Hill Road (Make left)
At 28.5, there's a stop sign. Is this deja vu? Turn left at the stop sign, staying on Route 113 south. There's Websters again.

### 29.4 East Conway Road (Stay straight)
At 29.4, you'll pass that familiar junction again by Sherman's. Stay straight as Route 113 makes way to East Conway Road.

### 35.1 Meeting House Hill Road (Make left)
Turn left on Meeting House Hill Road at 35.1. Enjoy the descent back to the parking area at 35.4.

# 20. Mount Clinton Road Loop

**EASY
12.3 MILES**

■ WHERE IS IT? Crawford Notch

■ SURFACE: Paved backroads

■ STARTING POINT: Trailhead for the Crawford Path.

■ DIRECTIONS: The trailhead is located .3 on the left side from the junction of Route 302 and Mt. Clinton Road in Crawford Notch.

■ FOOD AND STUFF: There's a convenience store along the way. Closest bike shops are in Littleton and Bartlett.

Crawford Notch is one of the most beautiful mountain passes in the White Mountains with its dramatic Presidential vistas. Not only that, the notch is a source of natural entertainment. In it, riders will find the origin of the Saco River (Saco Lake), the Appalachian Mountain Club's hostel, historical markers, hiking trails, a stop on the Conway Scenic Railroad and nearby attractions like the Mount Washington Cog Railroad, the Mount Washington Hotel and the Bretton Woods Ski Area. The Mt. Clinton Road loop is an easy, rolling ride with a bounty of rewards — including lots of downhill. The ride is best done on mountain and hybrid bikes. Some road bike riders might balk at the bumps and sand on Mt. Clinton Road in the early season. The road is not maintained year-round and winter's wrath is obvious. The ride is leisurely, with swimming opportunities available on the Base Station Road.

### 0.0 Start Crawford Path trailhead on Mt. Clinton Road
The trailhead is a fine starting point for the loop. Rest rooms

and a bench are there for your use. Leave the trailhead by turning left on Mt. Clinton Road and immediately pass a gate. Mt. Clinton Road will be your path for about 4 miles. It is shoulderless and a very low traffic area. The road rolls through the woods. A couple of clearings provide views of the mountains ahead. Streams rush by. Perhaps you can hear the trains in the distance. At about the 2.4 mile mark is a trailhead for Edmand's Path on the right. Enjoy the descent for about a half a mile, sweep right and slow down for the view of Mt. Washington right in front of you. There is a short pull after the downhill.

### 3.7 Junction with Base Station Road (Make left)

At the junction, riders should make a left on Base Station Road and prepare for the roller coaster. Also at that junction, riders could make a 1.5 mile side trip to the right to ride on the Cog Railroad. If riders were to go straight, it's a haul up through Jefferson Notch on a dirt road.

Base Station Road has a bit more traffic than Mt. Clinton Road, so pay attention. There is no shoulder. A stream rushes by and there are several pullouts to access the water for a cooling dip during the 5 mile stretch in the ride. You know you are at the end of the Base Station Road when you cycle past condos and see the grassy slopes of Bretton Woods. There is one final hill on  this road that appears larger than it really is. Don't be intimidated.

### 8.2 Junction Route 302 (Make left)

There is a stop sign here at the junction, a restaurant called Fabyans and a convenience store just beyond it. Take in the views of the Presidentials and ski area before riding on. It is here you turn left onto Route 302 which has a very wide shoulder. Those are the Presidentials in their grandeur. Cycle east. Take it easy over the diagonal railroad tracks and keep an eye out for a couple of churches — the white Shrine of Our Lady of the Mountains and the stone Episcopal Church with its fine stained glass windows.

At about the 9 mile mark, one of New Hampshire's grandest hotels comes into the view. The white lady with red roofs is the Mount Washington Hotel. There is a pullout with an historic marker. It is possible for riders to cycle to the hotel and take a

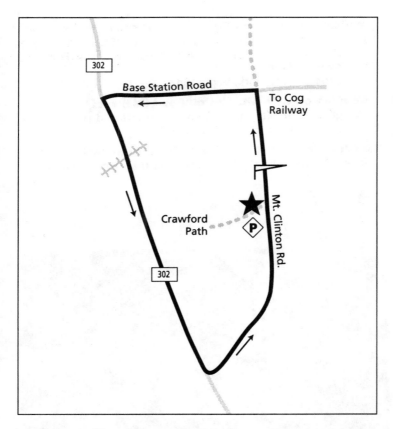

tour. If you do, look for the grandfather clock in the hall. Tradition has it that the first guest of summer and last guest of fall starts and stops it. Meander downstairs to the Cave, and slip back to another era.

After the ho-tel, pass through a 2 mile long stretch of ride that is known for its moose activity.

Well worth a stop at the 10.7 mile mark is the Eisenhower Wayside Park on the left. At first glimpse, it doesn't look like much. But, walk up the short trail and be treated to a vista and geography lesson. At the top is a sign which details the mountains you have been staring at during this ride. From left to right you see Mounts Jefferson, Clay, Washington, Monroe, Franklin, Eisenhower, Clinton and Jackson.

Near the 12 mile mark, begin the final ascent of the loop.

## 12.2 Junction with Mt. Clinton Road (Make left)

A sign tells of Mt. Clinton Road. Turn left and pedal a few hundred yards back to the starting point.

## 12.3 Junction with Crawford Path trailhead (Make left)

The ride ends where it began. Doesn't that bench look good?

# 21. Cherry Mountain Loop

**ADVANCED
25 MILES**

- ■ WHERE IS IT? Twin Mountain, near Bretton Woods
- ■ SURFACE: Forest Road/logging road/snowmobile trail/pavement
- ■ STARTING POINT: Trailhead for Lower Falls Hiking Trail
- ■ DIRECTIONS: From the I-93 side, the trailhead is located 3 miles east of Twin Mountain on Route 302 in the parking area 200 yards beyond the entrance to Zealand Campground.
- ■ FOOD AND STUFF: This is remote! Bring everything. Food and water is available after the ride at the convenience store by Bretton Woods and nearby Twin Mountain.

Maybe you'll see bear. Maybe you'll see moose. Maybe they'll see you. The Cherry Mountain Loop, in the shadows of the mighty Presidential Range, is a challenging and remote 25 mile adventure which offers stops at waterfalls, views of the Presidentials and the prize of having cycled over Jefferson Notch, the highest elevation state highway in New Hampshire.

Make no mistake about this loop. It's tough. There are sections, particularly along the Mt. Mitten Road, where advanced mountain biking skills are necessary. It also behooves you to brush up on your wildlife encounter skills. On this remote stretch of the loop, black bear cubs have been spotted scampering up trees and fresh moose tracks can be seen scattered throughout the wet, muddy sections.

There are long climbs as well. The trailhead parking lot is at an elevation of 1,506 feet and the ride crests at 3,009 feet. The climbs can be exhausting, and descents can be thrilling.

Terrain varies. The roads — Cherry Mountain Road and Jefferson Notch Road — are pleasant gravel and hardpack. The Mt. Mitten Road, and road is a very loose term here, can be grassy, muddy and rocky with tracts of singletrack. There are more scoops than in an ice cream shop.

Before embarking on the ride, be sure to have plenty of water. Carry a filter or purification tablets as there is no tap water available until the loop's end. Expect to spend a good portion of the day riding it too.

For bikepackers, there are primitive campsites along the way.

### 0.0 Start at trailhead on Route 302

Begin from the east side of the trailhead on the Lower Falls Hiking Trail. Head around the gate and enjoy the slight incline on the gravel road. The Ammonoosuc River parallels the road. At about the .5 mark, stop for a peak at the waterfall and horizontal, paper-like rock strata formations.

Soon thereafter, the road hits pavement. Those are the Presidentials in your face. Follow the pavement for about a half mile.

### 1.0 Junction (Turn left)

The road intersects with Old Cherry Mountain Road. Turn left on Old Cherry Mountain Road and cross the railroad tracks. As a landmark, a private camping area is on the right.

Old Cherry Mountain Road (Forest Route 14) is a steep and winding road. You will follow this road for 5.2 miles. There is about a mile of uphill before getting a break. Just a reminder — cars use it too. Though it is a low-traffic area, be aware.

The road continues up past trailers and small residences. Pass a gate and enter the White Mountain National Forest. Over the next several miles there will be 10 primitive campsites along Cherry Mountain Road.

### 3.6 Maybe moose

A sweeping right brings you to a roadside pond with a mountain vista. Look for the moose tracks in the muddy area.

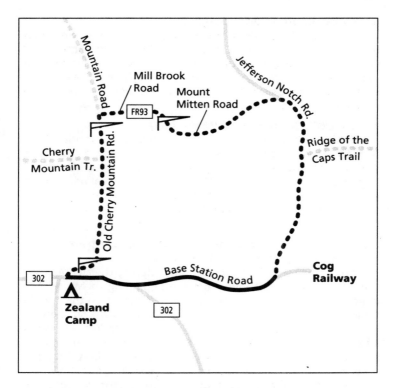

Start climbing again and prepare for a steep section. Don't fret. A break is coming up.

### 4.5 Cherry Mountain Hiking trailhead

When you get to the Cherry Mountain Hiking trailhead on the left with a parking area on the right, you have reached the top of Cherry Mountain Road (2,188 feet). The gated hiking trail is suitable for mountain bikers and it's about 3.5 miles to the top of the 3,544 foot Mt. Martha.

Now it's time for a steep and fast downhill with sweeping turns. Some of the stretch can be washboard. The descent lasts for about 1.7 miles. Pass by a gate and enter onto a section with summer homes.

## 6.2 Forest Road 93 (Make right)

Forest Road 93 or Mill Brook Road is a gated gravel road on the right. There is a stop sign on the left. Turn right here. Continue on the gentle road for just over a mile. Initially, the road descends. Then it's over a wooden bridge and nice views by a clearing. It winds some, crossing another wooden bridge and winds some more.

## 7.3 Gate/Mt. Mitten Road (Make left)

Mt. Mitten Road is the most remote section of this ride. There is a triangular sign with a bicycle   which points the way. Welcome to snowmobile country! The road is partially maintained by a snowmobile club. It begins as a gradual ascent with very grassy sections. The road will offer all sorts of challenges over the next 4.4 miles. Make the first short push and then stop to pick some berries.

## 7.8 Junction with three options (Take middle trail and look for triangular sign with bicycle)

Keep on eye out for mountain vistas during the clearings on the left. About a half mile from the beginning of Mt. Mitten Road is a junction with three trails. Make a right on the middle trail. There is a triangular sign with a bicycle pointing the way at this junction. The hard right is a snowmobile trail and is labeled such. Do not take that one. Take the second right or middle. You know you have taken the correct trail as there are signs indicating no snowmobiling is allowed. There is also a tree on the right with three blue horizontal stripes. Continue through this canopy of trees.

Oh, it was on this section of the loop that a baby black cub was once spotted up on a tree. Apparently, it was in the company of a larger relative. The larger relative was never seen. Just heard. This was a great motivator to press on at a faster pace.

## 8.2 Clearing

The gradual ascent continues into a clearing with wildflowers, dead wood and berries. From here, the climb increases in difficulty with some wet stretches and annoying tree branches at times. The trail is wide, though there are singletrack like parts until you reach a large, sweeping clearing.

### 9.1 Sweeping clearing

It's a bit wet with tall vegetation in here. Continue through the clearing and prepare for a tough stretch of just over a half mile with exposed metal drainage pipes, primitive bridges and mud. Moose like it here! After the obstacles, get ready for a steep descent through singletrack, rocks and mud. To help you get your bearings, on the far side of the clearing are snowmobile signs with arrows pointing the way, and one sign that says Mt. Mitten Road.

There are several orange blazes pointing the way during this stretch. In the high grass areas, pay particular attention as dips and drainages appear quickly.

### 10.9 Wooden bridge

The bridge, with its two low, log railings, is a place to rest. It crosses a stream where you can wipe away some of the mud you have accumulated on your bike and body. The good news is that the road mellows out considerably here.

### 11.7 Gate/End of Mt. Mitten Road

Mt. Mitten Road ends by a bridge, gate and rushing river. There are a couple of primitive campsites in the area.

### 11.7 Jefferson Notch Road (Make right)

When Mt. Mitten Road ends, Jefferson Notch Road begins. Make a right (orange signs point the way) and start another climb up a gravel road with about one-half mile of pavement. There are steep sections on the climb to 3,009 feet.

### 11.75 (Make right)

Almost immediately, make a second right (orange signs point the way). Remember, this is a road shared with other vehicles. As a landmark, there is a gated road in front of you. Ignore it. Climb. The road is steep, but hardpacked. Enjoy the rushing waters which run by its side. There are a few respites during the climb. Try and spot Mt. Jefferson through the trees.

### 13.0 Bear left at fork

Jefferson Notch Road forks after a paved section. Stay to the left and get back on the gravel for bit more of the grueling climb.

### 15.0 Caps Ridge Trail/Jefferson Notch sign

Nice job! You've just completed the 3.3 mile climb up Jefferson Notch Road. Get off the bike and snap a picture at the sign that says you are at 3,009 feet. Stretch those muscles in the Caps Ridge Trail parking lot. It's a 2.4 mile hike up Mt. Jefferson from there. Mt. Jefferson stands at 5,712 feet. Hikers climb to Mt. Washington at 6,288 feet from here too. Sometimes, friendly hikers will top off the water bottles of friendly bikers.

Get ready for a descent that will put smiles on after all those miles!

Go straight on Jefferson Notch Road. The Presidentials will be smack in your face. The descent on Jefferson Notch Road goes for 3.3 miles. It winds and is steep. Just after a half mile into the descent, the road banks sharply to the right. Pay attention.

### 18.3 Base Station Road (Make right)

The thrill will continue on the paved, shoulderless Base Station Road. For those interested, it's just 1.5 miles to the left to the Mt. Washington Cog Railway. But here, we make a right for a paved roller coaster ride along a river's edge for about 4.5 miles. When you start seeing townhouses and the grassy slopes of the Bretton Woods Ski Area, you know it's a sign that this is the beginning of the end.

### 22.8 Route 302 (Make right)

The stop sign brings you back to Route 302. A railroad bridge is on the left, a ski area in front of you and a restaurant and convenience store on your right. Finish the ride before heading to Fabyans for that beverage. Make a right for the last leg of the loop. The ride is smooth and the shoulder wide. There is a final descent into the parking lot on the right where all of this started.

### 24.9 Trailhead (Make right)

Make that last right back into the parking area. Go get that beverage!

# 22. Dolly Copp Thriller

**INTERMEDIATE
16 MILES**

- ■ WHERE IS IT? Gorham

- ■ SURFACES: Logging road, abandoned railbed, pavement, singletrack

- ■ STARTING POINT: Dolly Copp Campground, Gorham.

- ■ DIRECTIONS: Travel 4.5 miles south of Gorham on Route 16, or 18 miles north of Glen on Route 16. Park in the overflow area.

- ■ FOOD AND STUFF: Gorham has lots for the post-ride, and is passed through during this loop. Still, top off the water bottles.

Pinkham Notch is a favorite with hikers and skiers heading to Tuckerman Ravine and Mount Washington. A few miles from its high point is a ride that mixes up terrain with unsuspected views and climbs that both challenge and reward.

The Dolly Copp Thriller has a wide variety of terrain, including an unbelievably pleasant jaunt on an abandoned railroad bed with beautiful mountain views. The Dolly Copp Road, also called the Pinkham B Road, slices between Pine Mountain and Mount Madison and tops out at about 1,650 feet. Not maintained during winter, some of the road is packed dirt. Expect some vehicular traffic  and hikers on the road. The ride easily brings the rider out from civilization and back again. Even though the ride starts out on a climb, the 2.5 mile downhill prize comes quickly. Then the gentle railbed is ridden. Though the feel is that of being out in the middle of nowhere, the ride actually parallels Route 2.

After nearly 8 miles of off-road fun, the ride heads on pavement for a few miles and into the town of Gorham for a refreshing fuel stop. Riders then have the option of staying on pavement back to the ride's origin or test their skills and endurance back in the woods on the 5 mile long Bear Spring section of the ride which is both cruel — rough jeep road — and kind — downhill singletrack.

### 0.0 Start at Dolly Copp Campground parking lot.
Exit the parking lot.

### .1 Dolly Copp Road (Pinkham B Road) (Turn left)
Turn left onto the Dolly Copp or Pinkham B Road. The road is shoulderless and paved at this point. Soon, the pavement will undergo a few personality changes.

### .2 Intersection (Bear left)
There is a Y-intersection. To the right is the Barnes Field camping area. Bear left, the pavement turns to dirt and begin the ascent up the Dolly Copp or Pinkham B Road. After about a half mile of passing gated forest roads and heading up, the road changes back to pavement. Climb some more and a half mile later, presto, it's back to dirt. Near the 1.4 mark, the road starts to roll down.

### 1.6 Trailhead with Pine Mountain Trail
During this smile-producing descent, the road will return back to pavement at around the 2.4 mile mark and soon pass the Randolph town line. Zip down over several bridges and near the 3 mile mark, the road turns back to dirt and gravel. A half mile later, guess what? Back to pavement. The road enters by a clearing and several homes come into view.

### 3.7 Railroad crossing (Turn right)
The road crosses an abandoned Boston and Maine railroad bed that is part of a rails-to-trails program. Make a right here and go over the bridge. Be prepared for several bridge crossings over the next 4 miles.

The railroad ties have been pulled and the three percent grade down to Gorham is one of the most soothing and scenic rides in all of the White Mountains. Along this stretch of black

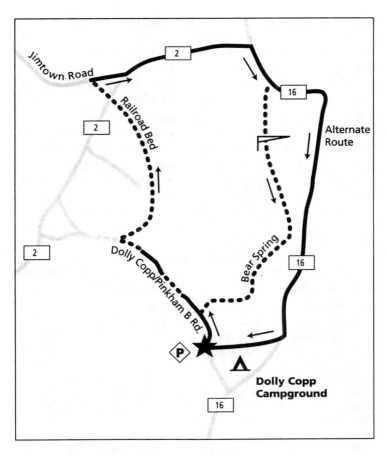

hardpack and gravel, look out for beaver dams and fowl which inhabit the marshy areas. The mountain views are serene. Pine Mountain stands 2,410 feet on one side while the Presidentials are in the distance. The Moose River flows alongside the trail for a spell, inviting riders to have a picnic or to cool off.

## 7.2 Pipeline clearing
The trail passes a clearing to an underground pipeline.

### 7.3 Overpass with Route 2 (go straight)
Continue straight at the four corners area and go underneath the overpass with Route 2. Homes will soon appear.

### 7.8 Jimtown Road (Make right)
Turn right on Jimtown Road. This is the road that will end the off-road experience for a while. Pedal about .1.

### 7.9 Route 2/Lancaster Street (Make left)
Turn left by the stop sign on Route 2, also called Lancaster Street. Continue for about 1.3 miles and head for the light.

### 9.2 Route 16 south/Route 2 east/Main Street (Make right)
At the traffic light, make a right on to Main Street in Gorham which is Route 16/Route 2. This easy haul through town is a place for refueling with all the restaurants and markets. There is a park at the opposite end of town with picnic tables for those looking for an al fresco experience.

### 10.6 Route 16 south (Make right)
Turn right on Route 16, go over the railroad tracks and start of the ascent up Pinkham Notch. The climb is gradual.

### 11.7 Wayside area for Bear Spring (Make right)
It's decision time. If you have grown accustomed to the pavement, stay with it for a nice gradual 5 mile ride back up to the Dolly Copp Campground. Just head south on Route 16 for 3.8 miles, passing the ranger information station (13.5 mile mark) and make a right at the sign for the Dolly Copp Campground, which is the Pinkham B Road (15.1 mile mark). Head .4 miles down and over the bridge to another Dolly Copp Campground sign. Make a left there and find your car. That's a total of 15.6 miles for the loop.

If there is still some kick in you, head for the Bear Spring section of this ride. Bear Spring is just over a 5 mile ride. Both rides end on a descent. The pavement is much easier than Bear Spring. For Bear Spring, turn right into the wayside area on the right side of the road. There is a sign which says "Adopt a Highway." There is a green post gate with a chain. Pass the gate, it's a right of way, and ride up into the clearing. The road will soon bear sharply to the right.

### 12.2 Forest Service gate
About a half mile from Route 16, there is a forest service gate. The logging road is a tad rough in sections and climbs.

### 12.4 Views
Some .2 later, look for the views off to the left of neighboring peaks. Head straight along the logging road. The road becomes grassy for a bit and heads into a clearing.

### 13.0 Junction (Bear left)
The road forks, and bear left. To get your bearings, a rusted delivery truck should appear on your right in a few turns of the pedal. In about .2, the area becomes very wet. It is best to walk your bike through this stretch. The ride becomes a bit technical with bridge crossings and rocks on the narrowing path.

### 13.8 Clearing
Exit the clearing at the far end to the left and get ready for a three-tenths of a mile singletrack downhill, with a nice curve and then short stream crossing. The downhill bottoms out in a sandy area.

### 14.1 Sandy area (Bear right)
Stay to the right at the sandy area and start to climb again for about a half mile before the road starts to roll again.

### 15.1 Clearing with views
Stop to soak in the scenery before rolling down the gravel and sweep around a big sand pit. The road enter back into the woods, becoming a well-packed logging road. The road is a roller coaster.

### 15.9 Forest Service Gate and intersection with Pinkham B Road (Make left)
Make a left past the forest service gate on the Pinkham B Road and enjoy the descent. You climbed part of this road earlier in the ride. Some .3 later, the road returns to pavement.

### 16.2 Intersection (Bear right)
Bear right at the Barnes Field Campground.

### 16.3 Dolly Copp Campground (Make right)
Turn right at the Dolly Copp Campground sign.

**INTERMEDIATE
18 MILES**

# 23. Bog Dam Road Loop

- ■ Where is it? Near Berlin
- ■ SURFACE: Logging road/pavement
- ■ STARTING POINT: Kilkenny Guard Station area
- ■ DIRECTIONS: From downtown Berlin, head northwest on Route 110 7 miles to York Pond Road (Berlin Fish Hatchery). Make a left and travel about 1.5 miles to the parking area by the Kilkenny Guard Station.
- ■ FOOD AND STUFF: Berlin and Gorham have the morsels and the bike shops. No water is available during the ride.

There is an area in the White Mountain National Forest which may well be more known by loggers, snowmobilers, fishermen and hunters than mountain bikers. Kilkenny is a prime timber harvesting spot, so it has an extensive logging road system (with hidden campsites) which can be used by bikers. Kilkenny is actually an unincorporated township, but the region lies among the communities of Berlin, Milan, Randolph and Stark. Perhaps even more so than Evan's Notch, this is an area which is the road less traveled. Though less than 10 miles from downtown Berlin, Kilkenny has a remote, wild feel to it. The nearly 18 mile-long Bog Dam Road loop is actually very close to the Berlin Fish Hatchery, which draws visitors to see the trout and salmon later stocked in the state's waterways.

Generally, the uphills on this ride are moderate, but it is the long downhills that make the trip worthwhile. With its canopy of trees, the ride is ideal on a hot day, with riders able to dip themselves into the headwaters of the Upper Ammonoosuc

River when the trip is over. The ride is marked well with mile posts.

## 0.0 Start

Bog Dam Road is also known as Forest Road 15. Pass the Kilkenny Guard Station, make a left and park in the area on the right side of the road.

Listen to the waters of the Ammonoosuc, hidden by the vast woods. Quiet will follow you on this ride. Head south on this clockwise loop. A few cranks of the pedal later, the river comes into view along the road and at the .3 mile mark an interpretive sign explains the area's habitat. This section of the ride is

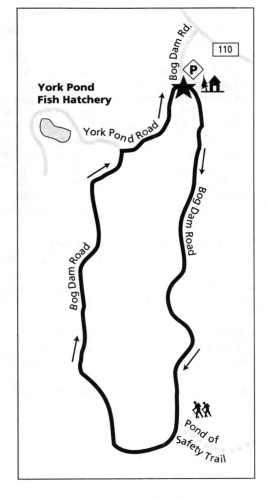

very gentle, the logging road a fine dirt path by river's edge.

The road leaves the river banks and slowly ascends, crossing One Mile Brook. The first hill hits here, and will get tougher over the next mile, before leveling off a bit.

Don't be lulled into complacency on this ride. Remember, this is a working forest and the road is open to motorized vehicles. Stick to the right.

At about 3.1 miles, a road to the Berlin Water Supply is crossed. Bog Dam Road rolls on and crosses the Upper Ammonoosuc hiking trail about a mile later. Though the area is thick with trees, try and catch a glimpse of the surrounding mountains through some of the thin spots from time to time.

Near the 8 mile mark, the Pond of Safety trailhead appears on the left. This is good news. For the most part, from here the road slopes downhill back to the parking lot. Now, there are a few spots to climb, but the toughest part is over. At 9.7, there is another crossing of the Upper Ammonoosuc Trail. A side trip is to ride the 3.2 miles to the Pond of Safety.

Near the 11.4 mile mark, the road rolls down again for about 3 miles.

### 15.3 York Pond Road (Turn right)

The fun doesn't end when Bog Dam Road does. At the 15.3 mile mark, turn right on the paved road. This is York Pond Road or Forest Road 13. It is shoulderless and also, rolls down gently. The sky opens up a bit on York Pond Road. The canopy of trees vanishes.

### 17.6 Bog Dam Road (Turn right)

Rather quickly, the Kilkenny Guard Station makes a return. When you see it, bang a right at the intersection with Bog Dam Road. The parking area is on the right. Those paths into the woods lead to the banks of the Ammonoosuc. Enjoy!

# 24. Pinkham and Evans Notches Loop

**INTERMEDIATE
84 MILES**

- ■ WHERE IS IT? Intervale

- ■ SURFACE: Pavement

- ■ STARTING POINT: Scenic Vista in Intervale, on Route 16/302.

- ■ DIRECTIONS: From North Conway, travel north a couple of miles on Route 16 to the Scenic Vista on the left.

- ■ FOOD AND STUFF: Good selection along the way for everything.

Two notches and two states await riders of this challenging, yet scenic 84-mile loop through New Hampshire and Maine. The notches pedaled through are like brothers. They share a last name, but each has its own personality. Pinkham Notch is dramatic as it cuts by the base of Mount Washington; rugged and wild with its treeless head exposed. Evans Notch acts as a natural border, snaking between the two states as it follows the Wild River with a tunnel-like canopy of trees overhead. Pinkham is wide open, while Evans is narrow.

Much of the terrain is hilly at the onset, with a few steep pulls through the notches. However, the ride also rolls through some of the flattest terrain in Mount Washington Valley along Route 113 into Fryeburg, Maine. Here, the road meanders along farms, quintessential New England homes and tiny towns. During this ride, there are many treats. The Jackson Covered Bridge, Mt. Washington Auto Road and the Shelburne birches are all passed. But perhaps the greatest treat is the Stowe store in Stowe, Maine at the junction of Route 113 and 113 B. It is here, many riders make the pilgrimage for the biggest kiddie ice cream cones in all of Stowe.

The ride does provide opportunity for food and water stops, but there are stretches where it will not be available for many miles.

In terms of road conditions, Pinkham Notch has a good shoulder most of the way while the Route 2 shoulder varies, and at times disappears. North Road is a wavy backroad and Evans Notch is narrow and winding with no shoulder.

The ride can be broken into an overnight adventure for touring. Motels and inns can be found in Gorham, and near Evans Notch in Gilead, Maine.

### 0.0 Start Scenic Vista, Intervale Route 16/302

The Scenic Vista is a roadside rest area with water, toilets, picnic tables and a commanding view of Mount Washington. Exit the area and turn left on Route 16 north/302 west, crossing the railroad tracks into Bartlett. The road has a wide shoulder. The Moat Mountain range will soon be on the left. The first of many hills, this one called Stanley's Hill, comes up at about 2.8 miles.

### 3.8 Junction of Route 16 and 302 (Make right on Route 16 north)

The road splits among the bustling intersection in Glen. Make a right at the light on Route 16 north and begin the climb up to Jackson, passing two attractions — Storyland and Heritage New Hampshire. A passing lane evolves after the attractions and stays for about a mile until the Jackson town line.

### 6.1 Covered Bridge

Stop at the red Jackson Covered Bridge. Lots of tourists take pictures there. You can too. Jackson is a splendid place, with galleries, lovely homes, inns, golf courses and a premiere network of cross-country ski trails.

The Ellis River makes an appearance along Route 16 as the climb continues. Don't worry. There is some relief and the road rolls a bit.

### 11.5 Pinkham Notch

Pinkham Notch welcomes you with a passing lane. If it's a clear day, look for the towers on top of Mount Washington in

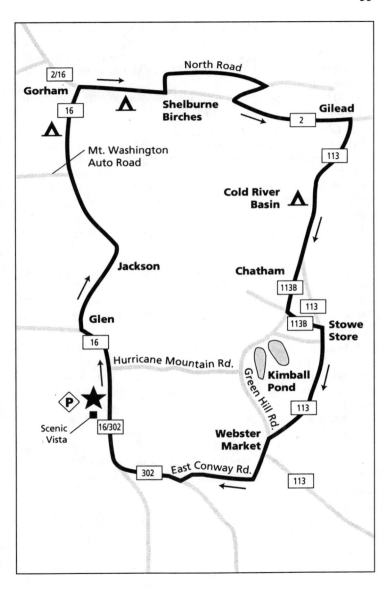

front of you. No, that's not another outlet store. That's the Mount Washington Observatory on the summit of the Northeast's highest peak at 6,288 feet. The climb up Pinkham Notch is not brutal. It is a four mile challenge, with plenty of wayside areas to rest.

At. 11.7, a sign welcomes you to the White Mountain National Forest.

## 16.0 Pinkham Notch Visitor Center

When you see the Appalachian Mountain Club's Pinkham Notch Visitor Center, you should be rolling downhill. The center, built in 1920, provides a starting point for many a hike up into the Presidentials. It is here, the famed climb to Tuckerman Ravine begins. The Appalachian Trail crosses here, and it's also a spot for water, bathrooms and more.

An historic sign up ahead will explain the first recorded ascent of Mount Washington by Darby Field. It's safe to say he didn't carry a titanium mountain bike up with him.

The Wildcat Ski Area comes up at 16.8. Once you pass that, get ready to cruise. You will see a sign all bicyclists love. That truck sloping downward. This one tells you of an eight percent grade for 1.7 miles. Check your brakes, put on the smile and ride on.

## 18.8 Mount Washington Auto Road

That's it, the climb up to the clouds. Once a year, the Auto Road is open to cyclists in an annual bike race. With an average grade of 12 percent, the road twists up 7.6 miles to a final pitch of 22 percent. The race is a lot of work for a t-shirt. Next to the Auto Road is a cross-country ski center called Great Glen Trails.

Enjoy the long rolling descent into Gorham.

At around 22.3, the road to the Dolly Copp Campground is passed and the road crosses into Gorham at the 22.8 mark. There is a White Mountain National Forest information center at 23.9 on the left.

## 26.8 Route 2 east (Make right)

Into Gorham you go. Watch out for the train tracks, and then make a right on Route 2 east which is also Main Street.

Gorham is a spot to re-fuel. There is a park at the corner of

Route 16 and Route 2 with picnic tables, as well as a convenience store. Fast food can be had in Gorham by turning left. This is the last opportunity for food for about 25 miles!

Gorham lies next to the city of Berlin, home to a paper mill. Logging trucks use Route 2. The views out of Gorham are pleasant. Pay attention to the diagonal train tracks at 27.4. Route 2 will start to roll up the further east you ride. There are a number of private camping areas. At about 38.8, enter into an area called the Shelburne birches. The white birches form a dazzling tunnel, particularly delightful in the fall.

### 30.3 North Road (Make left)

Turn left on North Road, a scenic, sweeping backroad in the northern White Mountains. Along the way, pass by a dam, see horses playing in fields and enjoy the clearings with mountain views.

### 34.2 Meadow Road (Bear right)

North Road intersects with Meadow Road. Bear hard to the right and the road opens up into a nice vista of the village of Shelburne with a church, park and bridge.

### 35.1 Route 2 east (Make left)

Turn left at the stop sign onto Route 2 again with its rolling terrain.

### 38.8 Maine state line

The road leaves New Hampshire and into Gilead, Maine.

### 41.0 Route 113 south (Make right)

Turn right on Route 113 and into Evans Notch. Route 113 acts as border between Maine and New Hampshire and crosses between the two states frequently. Route 113 parallels the Wild River and will have some nice downhill sections. The real climb begins some 6 miles later. At 43, enter the White Mountain National Forest again. The Hastings Campground is on the left at 44.4.

At 47, start the 2.5 mile climb up Evans Notch. Another sign with a truck at 49.5 will refresh you.

Enjoy the meandering two-mile descent.

### 51.7 Bricketts Place

On the left, Bricketts Place is a stop for information on the area.

### 52.0 New Hampshire state line

Route 113 heads into Chatham, New Hampshire. The Basin campground appears on the right. Soon thereafter, leave the White Mountain National Forest on the rolling road.

The ride opens up a bit with farms, summer homes, stonewalls, fields, cemeteries and views.

### 56.7 Route 113 B south (Make right)

Turn right on Route 113 B south after that big dipper and head for Center Chatham. Wind some more in this quiet, pretty area of rural New Hampshire. When you enter Center Chatham with its town house, church and historical museum it might appear you are the only ones in the area. Stay on Route 113 B south by bearing left here.

### 61.0 Route 113 south (Make Right)

At the stop sign, make a right on Route 113 south. But wait. That's the Stowe store, commonly referred to as "the mall." Head inside for ice cream, pastry and a most ecclectic wine and beer selection. Hang out on the deck. Watch life go by, slowly. Oh, you're back in Maine.

Route 113, at this point, is one of the more pleasant sections of the ride. Rural and rolling, it offers a glimpse of the road less taken. At 63, pass the town line for Fryeburg, Maine and roll into the small village of North Fryeburg with its school and chapel built in 1838. The road flattens out some around the 65 mile mark, passing the fields.

### 70.6 New Hampshire state line
### 70.7 Route 113 south (Make left)

At the stop sign, with Webster's Market in front of you, turn left and continue on Route 113 south.

### 71.7 East Conway Road (Continue straight)

There is a junction where Route 113 south heads left. Stay straight on East Conway Road. This is farm stand country. Sherman's farm stand will be on the left. The Nearfield farm stand will creep up on the right about a half mile later.

### 77.3 Junction with Route 302 west (Make right)

Turn right on Route 302 west by the Conway Police Station. The road enters Redstone, with its smattering of businesses. Those hills on the right are the Green Hills.

### 79.1 Route 16 north (Make right)

Turn right on Route 16 north. Yes folks, this is the famous "strip," filled with factory outlet stores, restaurants, hotels and attractions. At times, the "strip" can resemble a parking lot. Depending on the day and time of your arrival, you might actually be moving faster than the cars. There is also a chance the traffic won't be bad at all. The "strip" is relatively flat with the Moat Mountains on the right and Green Hills on the left. Mount Washington is in front of you. Pay attention to the traffic as many motorists make sudden turns without warning.

At 81.5, the "strip" becomes Main Street in North Conway with the green Schouler Park, yellow Victorian train station and little shops. About a half mile later, after the train trains, a wide shoulder returns and there is a bike lane for the last stretch of the ride.

### 83.6 Scenic Vista (Make left)

Hang a left into the Scenic Vista in Intervale.
Nice job!

**ALL LEVELS
8.8 OR 17.6 MILES**

# 25. Franconia Notch State Park Bike Path

- ■ WHERE IS IT? Franconia Notch

- ■ SURFACE: Paved bike path

- ■ STARTING POINT: Skookumchuck trailhead parking lot

- ■ DIRECTIONS: Drive north on Interstate 93 through Franconia Notch. Pass Cannon Mountain and bear east to Route 3. The trailhead is on Route 3 on the right.

- ■ FOOD AND STUFF: Cannon Mountain has a cafeteria and bike rentals. After the ride, Lincoln and North Woodstock have a lot of restaurants.

New Hampshire's most famous face resides in Franconia Notch. The Old Man of the Mountain lives in a neighborhood that will delight cyclists looking for a relaxing, easy ride with lots to do. The nearly 9 mile long bike path through Franconia Notch State Park is paved and offers riders a chance to explore an area between the towering peaks of the Franconia and Kinsman mountain ranges. It is here, cyclists can visit the New England Ski Museum, take a tram to the top of Cannon Mountain, walk into a gorge called The Flume, swim in Echo Lake, watch rock climbers, picnic and gaze upon the "Great Stone Face." This is an ideal ride for a picnic, as tables dot the ride. Binoculars are good idea too, especially by the cliffs near the Lafayette Campground.

For the most part, bikers share the path with pedestrians. There are two bike walk areas, and riders should follow those rules. Remember, this is an area where people are looking up at the sites. For maximum coasting, it is suggested to ride the path north to south. The northernmost terminus of the path is at the Skookumchuck Trailhead. Many people opt to start the ride from the parking lot at the Cannon aerial tramway where rental bikes are available and parking is ample. This would shave about 2.5 miles off the ride. Those with two cars, can park one at The Flume, then drive to the Skookumchuck and make a one-way trip.

Though the ride is easy, well-marked, and flat in sections, there are a few hills and curves. That said, enjoy.

## 0.0 Start Skookumchuck Trailhead

The Franconia Notch State Park Bike Path begins at the trail-head. It is well-marked. The ride will parallel the Franconia Notch State Parkway. Follow the signs and head south. Be prepared for the amazing vistas in the notch, one of grass-covered ski slopes, dramatic cliffs and soothing lake waters.

Near the 1.5 mile mark, look out from the Lafayette Brook Bridge Scenic Vista and then continue on the path as it rolls along the serene Echo Lake. Swimming, fishing and boating is possible in this lake, stationed at an elevation of 1,931 feet. There are the views of Cannon and Mt. Lafayette. Here, the water flows west to the Connecticut River.

Just after the 2.7 mile mark, the path leads into the parking lot of the aerial tram. There are several recreational opportunities. It is a five minute tram ride to the summit of Cannon at 4,200 feet. Up top is a summit observation tower and walking trails. Inside the base tram building is a gift shop, information center and cafeteria. Next to the tram is the New England Ski Museum. There is no admission charge to the museum.

Continue on the path to Profile Lake. The lake, below the Old Man of the Mountain, is the headwaters of the Pemigewasset River. Anglers try to fly-fish for trout. Viewing areas for the Old Man of the Mountain are evident. The Old Man is a natural rock profile estimated to be around 200 million years old, which gets nipped and tucked on an annual basis by a caretaker. There are five separate granite ledges that form the figure. If you look north from the Old Man, you may see a rock formation that look like the silhouette of a cannon barrel. That's how Cannon

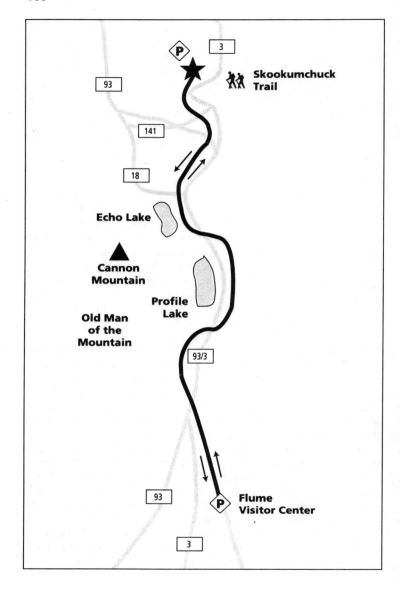

Mountain got its name.

Riding on, in no time you are at Lafayette Place, the camping and hiking hub of the notch. There are nearly 100 campsites here. The lodge offers a small history of the area. This is also a good spot to break out the binoculars.

Nearing the 7 mile mark, cyclists have the opportunity to view the Basin, a granite pothole formed by a waterfall. The pothole is some 20 feet in diameter and is believed to have formed some 25,000 years ago as the North American ice sheet was melting.

The end of the ride is at the 8.8 mile mark and The Flume. There is an admission charge into the gorge, but there is a free video presentation. There is an information center, cafeteria and gift shop here too. The Flume is a good place to rest up before the ride back. It is a natural gorge extending 800 feet at the base of Mt. Liberty. Discovered in 1808, the walls of granite rise up to a height of 70 to 90 feet and are from 12 to 20 feet apart.

**End**

To return to the Skookumchuck trail, follow the bike path.

**ALL LEVELS
19 MILES**

# 26. Beebe River Road/Sandwich Notch Road Loop

- ■ WHERE IS IT? Sandwich, near Waterville Valley
- ■ SURFACE: Logging road, dirt road, pavement
- ■ DISTANCE: Approximately 19 miles; a beginner ride is about 12 miles
- ■ STARTING POINT: Guinea Pond Trailhead on Sandwich Notch Road.
- ■ DIRECTIONS: From Interstate 93, take exit 28 and travel some 5.2 miles on Route 49 towards Waterville Valley and turn right on Sandwich Notch Road. High clearance vehicles are suggested for this road.
- ■ FOOD AND STUFF: A convenience store near Campton during the ride is good for re-fueling.

Want a ride that gives a remote feeling without going that far? This is it. The Beebe River Road is excellent for beginners, running along the banks of the river that bears its name. Cool your feet on a hot summer day or loll about for a picnic. It is relatively flat.

But intermediate riders and beyond usually want more, and combining a few paved backroads and Sandwich Notch Road makes for an excellent outing.

Just a note for motorists. Sandwich Notch Road is narrow and winding. Sometimes it seems best to travel it by bike or foot. Make sure your vehicle has high clearance or you might touch bottom.

### 0.0 Start Guinea Pond Trailhead

Leave the parking area and turn right on Sandwich Notch Road. Ride over the bridge spanning the Beebe River.

### .1 Beebe River Road (Turn left)

Make a left on Beebe River Road at the .1 mark. There is no sign. Beebe River Road follows along the banks of the river of the same name. There are numerous fire rings where people have camped and areas where the waters invite tired feet during the hot days of summer. The road is an old railroad bed and is a pleasure to ride, though there are spotty sections of rounded rocks and sand. This road calls for a picnic.

At about 1.2 miles there is a gate. Proceed past the gate, following the river. For the most part, the road is either level or a gentle decline as it heads west. Savvy riders will spot a trail on the other side of the river. It's a grassy snowmobile trail, not terribly inviting for mountain bikers.

The road leaves the tunnel of trees on occasion and opens up with power lines overhead.

Signs of logging are evident, and should there be a logging operation in progress, just use caution.

At about 5.8 miles, another gate is passed. Beginner riders should consider turning around and riding back to Sandwich Notch. The hills are about to begin. Don't fret, a nearly 12 mile ride is a fine outing too.

### 5.9 Eastern Corner Road (Turn right)

Make a right on Eastern Corner Road at about 5.9. There is no sign. But the dirt road heads uphill and soon passes homes, horses and a grassy clearing.

### 7.7 Page Road (Turn right)

Turn right on Page Road, by the yield sign, at about 7.7 miles. The dirt road offers some sturdy rollers by homes, crossing powerlines, after about a mile, heads back into the woods

### 9.9 Winter Brook Road (Turn left)

Turn left on Winter Brook Road and enjoy the ride down on pavement to Route 175.

### 10.5 Route 175 (Turn right)

Make a right on shoulderless Route 175 at about the 10.5

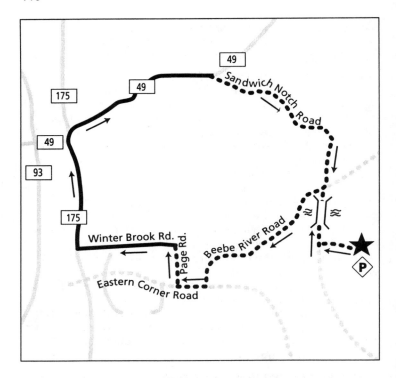

mark by the stop sign, and head north to Campton. There is a store here for those in need of refreshment.

### 11.1 Route 49 (Turn right)

At about 11.1, cross the bridge and make a right at the traffic light on Route 49 east. Admire the views of the pond and distant mountains. The shoulder returns.

Enter the White Mountain National Forest about a half mile later, and then there is a camping opportunity at the Campton campground.

### 14.2 Sandwich Notch Road (Turn right)

At about 14.2, make a right on Sandwich Notch Road and climb steeply. The road switches between pavement and dirt.

Enjoy the clearings and views after about a mile climb. This is but a brief respite for more climbing as you head back into the White Mountain National Forest. Near the 17.0 mark, look for the height of land sign on a tree on the left. Height of land is a patriotic 1,776 feet. There are some steep descents at this point and a stunning clearing. But don't smile too much, there are more steep climbs. Near the 19 mile mark, start the final downhill, zipping down past Beede River Road and over the one-lane bridge.

### 19.3 Guinea Pond Trailhead (Make left)

Turn left into the Guinea Pond Trailhead.

**INTERMEDIATE
51 MILES**

# 27. Ammonoosuc and Connecticut Rivers Loop

- ■ WHERE IS IT? Littleton
- ■ SURFACE: Paved country roads
- ■ STARTING POINT: Public parking area in Littleton, off Main Street.
- ■ DIRECTIONS: From Interstate 93, take exit 42 and turn right. Travel to Main Street, Littleton and make a left on School Street for the parking area.
- ■ FOOD AND STUFF: Food and water is available throughout the ride.

A half century is a fine goal for many cyclists while for others it is just another day in the saddle. This nearly 50 mile loop on the western slope of the White Mountains offers a look at some of the gentle valley's between the ranges. The beauty of this ride is in the fields of corn, farms and valley views along the banks of the Ammonoosuc and Connecticut Rivers. The Connecticut River Valley, which borders Vermont, offers up pastoral vistas with the sweet smell of agriculture. Route 135 from Woodsville to Monroe is the hilly showcase of this adventure that begins in the White Mountains, slips to the Connecticut River Valley region and comes on back to the Whites.

Small town New Hamsphire is served up on this one. From Main Street in Littleton to the oldest general store in America in Bath to cycling across the covered bridge in Woodsville, the loop is picturesque at its best and just a tad commercial at its worst. There is also the opportunity to visit the Moore Reservoir and stop at its picnic tables.

The ride heads through the communities of Littleton, Lisbon, Landaff, Bath, Haverhill, Woodsville and Monroe.

The shoulder ranges from excellent to non-existent. The loop can be done in either direction. In this direction, the rural beauty of Monroe is saved for last.

### 0.0 Start Main Street, Littleton

Leave the School Street parking lot and head west by making a right. This is Main Street.

### .4 Blinking light  for Routes 302/10 (Bear left)

At .4, bear left at the blinking yellow light on Routes 302/10. The road heads through a fast food alley, crosses over Interstate 93 and will soon widen out a bit. Routes 302/10 is a rolling road for the most part. Near the 3 mile mark the Ammonoosuc River comes into play.

Cycle through the valley. Antique shops might call out your name. Depending on the season, stop for fresh vegetables from corn to squash.

There is a campground at the 6.7 mark. Near 10 miles, the ride approaches the town of Lisbon. There's another campground here too. In Lisbon, a small factory town, opportunity exists for re-fueling.

After Lisbon, the road starts to wind up to the town line of Landaff. The short burst into Landaff is followed by Bath, a tiny picturesque spot worth stopping for a spell. First, there is a short steep hill to conquer after a row of brick homes. Then, roll smack down into the center of town at about the 16.8 mark.

Stop in Bath. Head into the Brick Store, usually draped with an American flag. Walk down to the Bath Covered Bridge. Cruise by town hall, built in 1910, or the church, 1873. There's a place for ice cream too. Enjoy this fine corner of the world.

Roll on.

At about the 18 mile mark, there's another climb of about a half mile. Then the road meanders towards Woodsville.

### 20.8 Blinking yellow light with Route 302 (Make right)

Up the hill at the 20.8 mark is a blinking light, make a right here on Route 302 west. More opportunity for re-fueling is available in Woodsville, with its nice little dip into town.

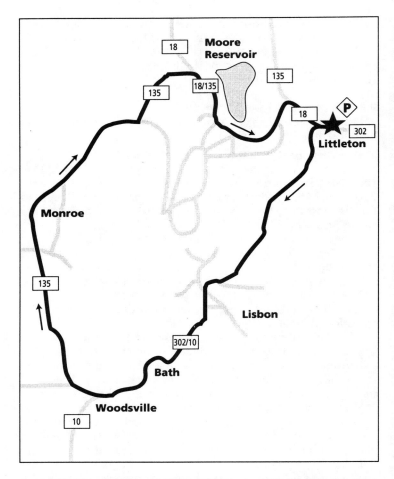

## 21.8 Blinking yellow light with Route 135 (Make right)

Turn right at the blinking yellow light onto Route 135 and head north for Monroe. Cycle over the Haverhill-Bath Covered Bridge, built in 1827.

Sweeping turns and views are your rewards on this backroad. The road becomes very hilly and offers vistas into Vermont.

There isn't much of a shoulder, but traffic is low. Some of the hills are very dramatic in both the uphill and downhill.

Cycle into Monroe at about the 30 mile mark. There is a store here.

Out of Monroe, head up again and at the top of the hill check out those views before zipping back down.

Once you get to the Maple Hill Farm, you just finished a mile climb. That's about the 35 mile mark. There will be more rolling hills.

Near the 39 mile mark, you'll see signs indicating sharp downhills, including one of about 2 miles. Enjoy! But remember, what goes down, must come up.

Just after the 43 mile mark, the Moore Reservoir is passed. There is a visitor center. Soon thereafter, a state rest area with bathrooms, phone booths and information center comes into view. The road turns into 135 north/18 south. Big hills await.

### 48.6 Intersection with Route 18 south (Make right)

After that thrilling downhill, be sure to stop at the stop sign. This is an intersection with Route 18. Turn right for the final leg into Littleton.

### 50.3 Intersection with Routes 302/10 at blinking light (Make left)

Turn left and it's back on Main Street.

### 50.7 Intersection with School Street (Make left)

Turn left on School Street to parking.

**ALL LEVELS
18.5 MILES**

# 28. Campton Bog Road Ramble

- ■ WHERE IS IT? Campton, Rumney
- ■ SURFACE: Dirt road/Backcountry road
- ■ STARTING POINT: Small parking area by Blair Covered Bridge.
- ■ DIRECTIONS: From I-93, exit 27, make left. At blinking yellow light, go straight to covered bridge.
- ■ FOOD AND STUFF: Bike shops and food are in Plymouth. There's a convenience store in Rumney.

If there ever was a competition for the funniest sign on a covered bridge, the Blair Covered Bridge in Campton should be in contention. It says "five dollars fine for riding or driving on this bridge faster than a walk." The sign sets the tone for this pleasant country ramble through Campton, Rumney and Plymouth in the foothills of the White Mountains. Combining dirt roads and backroads, the mostly gentle circuit takes the rider on tree-shaded Campton Bog Road as it winds past small farms, stone walls and rustic homes. There are several hills on this road, but the reward is quickly felt on the tail end of the route.

After dirt, the journey leads to quintessential, low-traffic backroads which provide mountain, field and farm views. Ride past the grassy runway of the Plymouth Municipal Airport. Stop for a yard sale or by a farm stand.

### 0.0 Start Parking area by Blair Covered Bridge, Blair Road

Leave the bank of the Pemigewasset River by heading for the

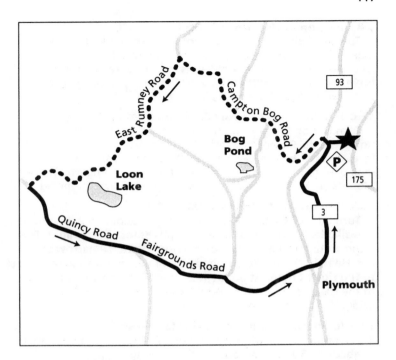

blinking yellow light and stop sign at the intersection of Route 3 and Blair Road. Continue straight past the light as the road now becomes Campton Bog Road. Head under the overpass and bear to the left. The road is pavement at this point. The interstate is soon left behind.

Campton Bog Road winds and rolls upward as it turns to dirt at about the 3 mile mark.

Campton Bog Road holds a couple of surprises. Though it predominately is through the woods, a couple of times it opens up to glorious fields where the old (barns, stone walls, farm equipment, etc.) meets the new (satellite dishes). One such surprise is at about the 3.3 mile mark. The road climbs a bit, but there is a nice descent that goes nearly 3 miles.

Somewhere along the way Campton Bog Road undergoes a name change to East Rumney Road.

### 9.8 Junction with Quincy Road (Make left)

Turn left on the paved Quincy Road at about the 9.8 mile mark. There is no shoulder, but that's okay. The road is fairly level. Take in the scenery of farms and mountains, crossing the town line into Plymouth at about 11 miles. Cycle past the airport and then to a junction with pleasing fields.

### 12.0 Junction with Fairgrounds Road (Make left)

Turn left on Fairgrounds Road at about the 12 mile mark. It's right next to Plymouth Sands Camping Area. Farms and fields forever could be the mantra on this gentle road. At about 13.2, look over to the mountains and see the slopes of nearby Tenney Mountain. At about 14 miles, the fairgrounds are on the left.

### 15.2 Junction with Route 3 (Make left)

Turn left on Route 3, heading north, at about 15.2. Fast food is available. Route 3 also has several places for an overnight. This is the more commerical side of the ride. There is a narrow shoulder. Head back into Campton about a mile later and wind back to the ride's origin. At about 17.3, there is a fine vantage point of the rocky shores of the "Pemi," complete with an old railroad bridge for the backdrop.

### 18.5 Junction with Blair Road (Make right)

Turn right at the blinking yellow light back on to Blair Road at about 18.5 and head back to the parking area.

# 29. Ellsworth Pond Loop

**INTERMEDIATE
6.3 MILES**

- ■ WHERE IS IT? Ellsworth
- ■ SURFACE: Forest road/dirt road/singletrack/snowmobile trail/pavement
- ■ STARTING POINT: Ellsworth village.
- ■ DIRECTIONS: From I-93, exit 27, make left. At blinking yellow light, left on Route 3 north. Travel 2.7 miles to Dan Web Road and make left (following signs to Stinson Lake and Ellsworth). Then left on Ellsworth Hill Road. Travel 4.5 miles to Ellsworth with white church and white town house. Limited parking available by town house by making right on Ellsworth Pond Road.
- ■ FOOD AND STUFF: Bring both food and water as there is nothing along the ride. There is a general store by Stinson Lake en route to the start of this ride.

Ellsworth has no police, no store, no post office, no fast food. It is small town New Hampshire and offers a fun and furious 6.3 mile intermediate loop. You've got to smile on this one. Head over to the town house/old school house built in 1814. Maybe they'll still have a newspaper article or two in the display case outside. Then, take a walk over to the church and look behind it. How many churches have you been to with an outhouse?

Sights aside, the ride has a lot of different terrain in a very short amount of mileage.

Most of this ride is easy, but on the tail end, there's a burst up

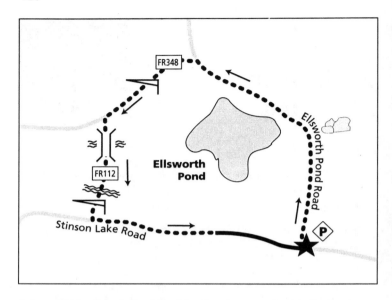

Stinson Lake Road. But the big dip down ends this little zinger on a very positive note.

## 0.0 Start Ellsworth Pond Road

The dead end sign leads the way on the dirt Ellsworth Pond Road. The ride begins on a downhill smack through what could be considered downtown Ellsworth. There's even a sort of monument in the middle of town. About .15 miles into the ride, the road bears to the left at the Ellsworth rock. On it, the name of the town is inscribed and the date 1769.

Near the .75 mark, Ellsworth Pond is seen through the trees on the left as small homes are passed.

## 1.3 Forest Road 348 (Make left)

At 1.3, turn left on the road leading to Forest Road 348. There is an arrow here. One-tenth of a mile later, pass a forest service gate. The terrain rolls upward at this point.

## 2.2 Snowmobile Trail (Make left)

Near 2.2 the forest road ends in a clearing. Make a left by the arrow and head over the wooden bridge on a snowmobile trail. After the bridge, enjoy some fine singletrack for a spell. The trail heads uphill. Pass a couple of signs near the 2.4 mark. One points straight for Stinson Lake Road while the other indicates the way to Ellsworth Pond. Stay straight and continue up the hill, riding over the occasional old log. The climb stops at about 2.7 and then it's time to ride down. Near the 2.9 mark, there is a Y. Bear left on the singletrack and head down the pitch to a clearing.

### 2.95 Forest Road112 (Make right)

At the 2.95 mark, make a right on Forest Road 112. It is not marked. To get your bearings, you'll soon cross over a bridge. This forest road is beautiful doubletrack. Pass a wooden gate near the 3.5 mark and sweep around the corner. Near 3.9, there is a stream crossing. The bridge was not in place during the autumn of 1997, so use the rocks if the span has not been replaced. Pedal ahead to the forest road gate and go around it.

### 4.0 Stinson Lake Road (Make left)

Near the 4 mile mark, turn left on the well-packed dirt Stinson Lake Road. The road is smooth. Head up the hill. There will be a couple of rollers, including a half mile stint to the top. During the descent, the road will return to pavement. There is also a huge dip with a pitch of 15 percent. Enjoy the surrounding vistas and rolling past the old cemetery, but prepare to end your ride at the bottom of the dip.

### 6.3 Ellsworth Pond Road (Make left)

At 6.3, turn left on Ellsworth Pond Road to end the ride. Stroll over to the graveyard and have a peak at history.

**INTERMEDIATE
40 MILES**

# 30. Kinsman Notch Loop

- ■ **WHERE IS IT?** North Woodstock

- ■ **SURFACE:** Pavement

- ■ **STARTING POINT:** North Woodstock municipal parking area on Morris Street which is off Route 3

- ■ **DIRECTIONS:** Take exit 32 from Interstate 93 and turn right. Morris Street is near the Route 3 traffic light.

- ■ **FOOD AND STUFF:** Food and water is available during the ride.

One of the most scenic and satisfying road rides in the western White Mountains is this nearly 40 mile loop through North Woodstock, Easton, Franconia and Lincoln. The ride does tackle the long, slow climb up Kinsman Notch and the shorter but steeper ascent of Mittersill Hill. The route also meanders along the banks of Moosilauke Brook, through a pastoral valley floor and has engaging downhills.

For the most part, the pavement is fine on this ride which incorporates Route 112, Route 116, Route 18, a portion of the Franconia Notch State Park Bike Path, Route 3 bike lane and Route 3. The shoulder varies along the way.

Food and water is available throughout the ride, and there are a number of reasons to get off the saddle to explore the area. The ride should be topped off at one of the many eateries in the Lincoln/North Woodstock area.

## 0.0 Start North Woodstock municipal parking area on Route 3

Leave the parking area, heading for the lights at the intersection of Routes 3 and 112.

## .1 Traffic light intersection (Make right on Route 112)

At the traffic light, turn right on Route 112, heading west.

Route 112, also called Lost River Road, winds along the Moosilauke Brook. The road rises gently at first, passing the Woodstock town offices, private camping areas, and homes. As civilization appears to peter out, the grade increases through Kinsman Notch and in reality, the total climb will be about 5 miles. Enter the boundary for the White Mountain National Forest at about 4.1 and at the 4.7 mark, a passing lane materializes which is a harbinger for the climb ahead. For resting purposes, there are a couple of wayside areas during the ascent, but all are on the left-hand side of the road.

The height of land is reached near the entrance to Lost River, an attraction featuring a gorge and cave. This is about the 5.8 mile mark.

Get in cruising position after this point because you are about to fly.

The shoulder improves and the ride goes through one of the more beautiful parts of the forest. If you can stand stopping, consider looking around Beaver Pond at about the 6.3 mark. There are bathrooms at the trailhead, and here the road crosses the Appalachian Trail. There is also a sign foreshadowing the terrain ahead — nine percent grade for the next 2 miles.

The road and shoulder will narrow as you approach the town line of Easton at about 8.6. Route 112 winds through this area and snakes by the Wildwood camping and picnic area at about 8.9.

## 11.3 Junction with Route 116 (Make right on Route 116)

Say good-bye to Route 112 by making a right on Route 116, heading north. Route 116 will be your route for the next 11 miles. The road rolls along, with the more challenging hills at its onset. But as the ride progresses closer to Franconia, the terrain is more rolling and enters a spectacular area of farms, inns and vistas. Leave the White Mountain National Forest at about 14.3 and some 2 miles later pass the Easton town offices. Pass the Fraconia town line at 18.3 and marvel at the scenery. The upcoming Franconia Aiport, with its gliders, is well worth a stop

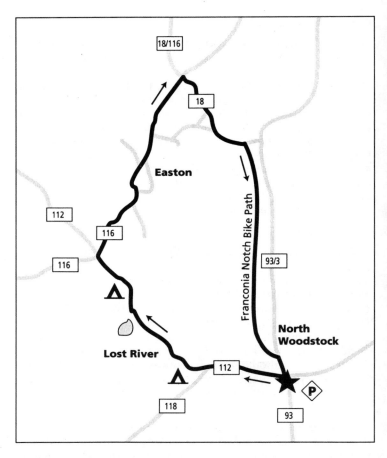

if the planes are active. About a mile later, there is an opportunity to visit the Robert Frost Museum.

### 22.7 Junction with Route 18 (Make right on Route 18)

Franconia, mid-way through the loop, is a good resource for food and water. Turn right on Route 18, heading south. After a lazy spin through Franconia, Mittersill Hill screams at about the 25.2 mark. This has steep sections.

Top out at about 26.6. Route 18 then passes the Mittersill Alpine Village, a Swiss-style area with lovely chalets set on the slopes of the dormant Mittersill ski area, adjacent to Cannon Mountain. The road dips here and that's the end of the tough climbs on this ride. It would be too broad of a statement to say it's now all downhill from here, but it's pretty damn close.

At about the 27.2 mark, pass the Peabody Lodge of Cannon and get ready to head onto the bike path.

### 27.6 Junction with Bike Route (Make right)

Turn right by the Bike Route sign at the 27.6 mark. This is the Franconia Notch State Park Bike Path. There are several reasons to stop along the path — tram, ski museum, Old Man of the Mountain, bathrooms, water, snacks, etc. Follow the bike path until it ends, just over 6.5 miles.

### 34.2 Junction with Route 3 (Make left)

The bike path will end in a parking lot for The Flume. Exit the parking lot and turn left on Route 3 south. The downhill sensation will continue as you leave Franconia Notch State Park and head into the strip of attractions, motels and restaurants of Lincoln. Route 3 has a nice wide shoulder which evolves into a bike lane. Pass the town line of Woodstock at about 38.5 and then enter the charm of North Woodstock.

### 39.2 North Woodstock Municipal Parking Area

This is where it began. Go get something to eat.

**ALL LEVELS
6 MILES**

# 31. Lincoln Woods Trail

- ■ WHERE IT IS? Lincoln
- ■ SURFACE: Logging road/Forest road
- ■ STARTING POINT: Lincoln Woods trailhead.
- ■ DIRECTIONS: I-93, exit 32, 4 miles east on Route 112, Kancamagus Highway to Lincoln Woods trailhead.
- ■ FOOD AND STUFF: There are plenty of food opportunities in Lincoln before and after the ride, but nothing during it. Bike shops are there too.

One of the easiest and most scenic mountain bike trails in the entire White Mountain National Forest is the Lincoln Woods Trail in Lincoln. The trail is an old logging railroad that was last operational in 1948 and follows the East Branch of the Pemigewasset River. This trail is a heavily-used corridor by both hikers and bikers. It is the central artery for a number of paths which head into the Pemigewasset Wilderness, an area where bicycles are forbidden. It is not uncommon to see kids with fishing poles, parents with backpacks, youths on overnights and day walkers all using the trail. There are spots to cool off in the river too. Due to its popularity, cyclists must be courteous. Pass hikers with care, and use a friendly and proper warning.

The Lincoln Woods trail is ideal for families. A trip out and back to the wilderness boundary is nearly 6 miles. Riders will cycle over a suspension bridge and have the opportunity to add a short walk to a waterfall as part of the experience.

More adventuresome riders can wet their feet by crossing the river and making a loop back via a forest service road on the eastern bank. This is also an approximately six mile circuit. This section will cover both rides.

The Lincoln Woods parking area is well-serviced with bathrooms, nearby camping and an information center. Since crossing the river in high water is extremely dangerous, those riders thinking of doing the loop should stop in to the center for the latest conditions, and suggestions from park rangers.

Riders take note. Though the trail is of the gentlest grade, many of the old railroad ties remain. Instead of riding over them, it is possible to ride to either side. Every once in a while, there are small, wooden bridges to cross.

## 0.0 Start trailhead

The ride begins directly in front of the porch of the information cabin. To eliminate carrying your bicycle down the stairs, ride the service road a few feet and make a left at the junction. The suspension bridge will come into view. Cycle over the bridge which crosses the East Branch.

## .10 Junction (Make right)

After crossing the bridge, make a right. The wide trail follows the waters, sometimes leaving its edge, only to return again. At about the 1.4 mile mark, the Osseo Trail is on the left, while at the 2.6 mile mark the Black Pond Trail is crossed. At about the 2.8 mile mark, the Franconia Brook campground is visited.

## 2.9 Trails end (for beginners)

The trail, at least for cyclists, nears its end at the 2.9 mile mark. There is a stone structure here where many hikers gather to rest or eat during a trip. Cyclists can cross the bridge behind the stones, but nearly immediately after the bridge, the wilderness area begins. Trails end is a good spot for a lunch. From here, it is possible to take a short .4 mile walk to Franconia Falls. This is highly recommended. Just follow the sign. Cyclists can leave and lock their bikes here.

It is here, beginners should return to the parking area along the Lincoln Woods Trail, enjoying the same path from a different perspective.

Better riders can continue the loop with a river crossing.

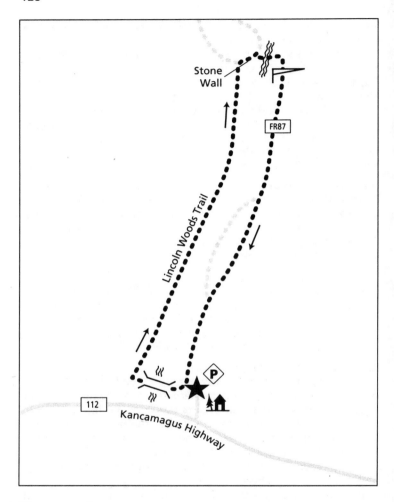

## River crossing

Riders will cross the river twice to get to the other side. Begin by heading back along the Lincoln Woods trail for about 30 feet. On the left is a path. Make the left and follow it down to the banks of the river. Look across the water and see another path through the trees. This is the destination. Carefully cross the river.

On the other side, follow the path around to the right and a sandy beach. The Forest Service usually constructs a primitive stone bridge for hikers to walk across. The bridge acts as a guide for bikers. Carefully cross the river to the path on the other side.

Ride up the path.

### 3.1 Service Road (FR 87) (Make right)

Make a right on the service road (FR 87), bounded by a gate to the wilderness area. The service road is a bit of a dipsy-doodle through the woods. It is well-maintained, but there are a couple of spots with rough gravel. Some .3 later a fine viewing area, bordered by several large boulders, is passed. The road rolls up to a ridge, up over the river near the 5 mile mark. Then, just run with the waters and look for the swimming holes.

### 5.9 End

The ride ends by the suspension bridge first crossed in the beginning of the loop.

**ALL LEVELS VARIES**

# 32. Livermore Road/ Greeley Ponds Trail

- ■ WHERE IS IT? Waterville Valley
- ■ SURFACE: Forest road/logging road
- ■ STARTING POINT: Livermore Road trailhead in Waterville Valley.
- ■ DIRECTIONS: To get there, take exit 28 off I-93 and travel on Route 49 to Waterville Valley. Turn left onto Tripoli Road, then bear right at the "Y" after a mile. Turn right a half mile later on West Branch Road. The parking area is over the bridge.
- ■ FOOD AND STUFF: There's food and a bike shop in Waterville Valley's Town Square. Food and water is available at the gas station on Tripoli Road too.

Livermore Road is a pleasure for all outdoor lovers. Hikers use it as an access point to four thousand footers like Mount Tripyramid while others just use it for jogging or walking. Mountain bikes are welcome too. Livermore Road is the perfect spot for a bike n' hike adventure. Don't forget the picnic too. With short walking paths off the road inviting exploration, the area is a good spot for families looking for an easy adventure.

Livermore Road also offers the intermediate and advanced mountain biker the chance to tackle tougher terrain by accessing the Greeley Ponds Trail which follows an old logging road for about a mile and ends at the ponds which are located in a notch between Mount Kancamagus and the East Peak of Osceola.

In essence, the road and its side chutes are a bit of an all-terrain mountain bike park. Bikers can try all sorts of terrain like smooth dirt, single track and double track. Though Livermore Road appears as a wide, flat carpet at the beginning, it does offer a long climb and change of terrain before petering out to the Livermore Trail after the 5 mile mark. A ski trail in winter, Livermore Road once linked Waterville Valley to the Sawyer River logging railroad which led to the now deserted village of Livermore on Sawyer River. For now, it's a road that connects bikers to fun.

Not all the paths leading off Livermore Road are suited for mountain bikes. Those concerned about the safety of their bicycles should consider locking them together before heading out for the scenery.

The description for Greeley Ponds follows the narrative of the paths off Livermore Road.

### 0.0 Start Livermore Road Trailhead

Leave the parking area by the sign board, ride through the boulders and hook up to the left with Livermore Road. The road's best surface is found for the first 3 miles as it gradually winds its way upward. The road goes over a bridge spanning the Mad River and offers several fine views of the surrounding peaks.

### .5 Boulder Path

For those riders looking to bike and walk, the first stop on the tour is the Boulder Path. It is out on the right and leads to a massive boulder in Slide Brook.

### .7 Big Pines

The Big Pines Trail, on the left, is not a good place to ride a bike. The trail is about a quarter-mile hike to, you guessed it, big pines.

### .9 Kettles Path

The melting ice from glaciers formed the giant basins here on this easy walk. Though it looks inviting for mountain bikes, the path will soon not be rider-friendly.

### 1.8 Norway Rapids

The trail, very close to the road, leaves on the right. Don't

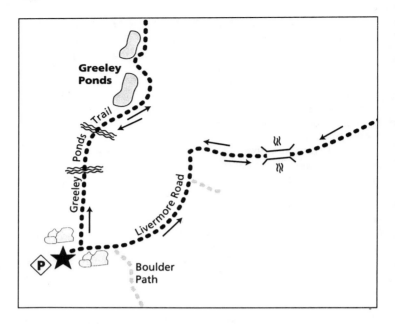

bother bringing the bike. But enjoy gazing at the layers of rock.

From here, the easy walks disappear and the hiking begins. Riders can continue upwards, crossing by the junction with Snow's Mountain Road at about 2.1 miles and then the clearing by Avalanche Camp at about 3 miles. It is at this mark that the road surface starts to deteriorate somewhat, and becomes rougher with double track as it swings to the left during a hair-pin turn. The road becomes steeper and gradually becomes the Livermore Trail, a path only for those who enjoy putting their bikes in their backpacks.

Ride as long as you like, and turn around for the exhilarating downhill back to the parking lot.

## GREELEY PONDS TRAIL - Ride out from the Livermore Road Trailhead.
### .3 Junction with Greeley Ponds Trail (Make left)

Turn left at the sign at .3 for the Greeley Ponds Trail. It is here the trail follows an old logging road. After being on Livermore Road, the road seems a lot rougher. Instead of smooth, it is a bit rocky in sections. There will be several bridge crossings during the course of this ride. Also, it can be a wet, muddy one depending on the season. Roots tend to get in the way too.

Then why ride it?

The ponds, in a scenic area, are well worth a look, and the ride back down will give a you an appreciation for the effort you make while climbing.

Follow along the Mad River, in the shade of the trees. The Scaur Trail is passed at .7 while the Goodrich Rock Trail makes an appearance at about .9. After about a mile, the trail leaves the logging road, crossing the river yet again. Singletrack makes a brief showing before rocks and roots take over. Smooth sections also appear as the ride gradually heads upward. At 1.2, say hi to the Flume Path.

## 2.5 Junction over Mad River (Make left)

At about 2.5, the trail crosses the Mad River for the final time. It's decision time. Make a left.

But, what about the bicycle? You can leave it here, or brave about a quarter mile of push, pull and carry to the first pond.

After gazing upon the waters, head back and enjoy the fruits of your efforts.

INTERMEDIATE
10 MILES

# 33. Skookumchuck Loop

- Where is it? Franconia Notch
- Surface: Snowmobile corridor, forest roads
- Starting point: Skookumchuck trailhead parking lot.
- Directions: Drive north on Interstate 93 through Franconia Notch. Pass Cannon Mountain and bear east to Route 3. The trailhead is on Route 3 on the right.
- Food and stuff: There is nothing along the way. The nearest would be the cafeteria at Cannon Mountain.

The Skookumchuck Loop is a dynamic blend of paved bike path, well-marked snowmobile trail, forest road, overgrown paved road and Route 3. There is ample downhill, and the overgrown section of Old Route 3 is a unique sampling of terrain. The growth gives the illusion of singletrack and slickrock all rolled into one.

This ride includes a fun roller coaster hairpin turn, plenty of bridge crossings and nearly 2 miles of climbing. For those unnerved by the thought of that climb, do not be intimidated. If there ever was a ride that gives you quadruple return on your investment, this is it.

### 0.0 Start at Skookumchuck Trailhead
Head south on the paved bike path.

### .2 Turn left on Corridor 11 snowmobile trail
The ease of the bike path is soon left for the adventure of the Corridor 11 snowmobile trail through the woods. There is a sign

on the lefthand side and shows arrows to Twin Mountain and Bethlehem. Make that left and start the climb.

The snowmobile trail is well-marked. There are arrows and caution signs along the way. The caution signs usually indicate a bridge is ahead.

The wide trail can be a tad steep at times and the terrain offers dirt, rock and hay. Just after the .3 mark into the ride, there is the first of many bridge crossings over the next mile and half or so. During the climb, there are brief respites where the trail levels off and even rolls. The dips can be exhilarating.

Near the 2.3 mile mark is a wide, sweeping banked turn over a bridge. From here, the return on the investment begins.

The trails now snakes down. There is a hairpin curve and then the trail winds downhill As you descend, the trail becomes more grassy.

### 3.1 Junction with big boulder (Make left)

The trail comes to a T. Make a left onto an unmarked forest service road.

### 3.3 Junction (Make right)

After .2, there is another junction. Make a right and continue to descend on a well-defined forest road (92A) Let gravity do the work and meander on down.

### 4.4 Gate (Make left)

After the gate, make a left. This is Gale River Road. The downhill continues on a hardpack service road with limited, primitive camping. There will be several bridge crossings as the road parallels the river. At about the 4.7 mark, the first bridge is crossed. Look for the well-worn foot path just after it on the right side and follow it to a local swimming hole. Just for bearings, at about 5.3 miles there is a sign signifying the Littleton water supply.

### 5.5 Gate (Make sharp left on Old Route 3)

By the time this gate is reached, you might hear the sounds of Route 3. If you reach Route 3, you've gone too far. Make a hard left and ride between the three large boulders.

This is Old Route 3. It is a mishmash of terrain and a real hoot. At about the 6 mile mark there is a gradual incline up a ridge

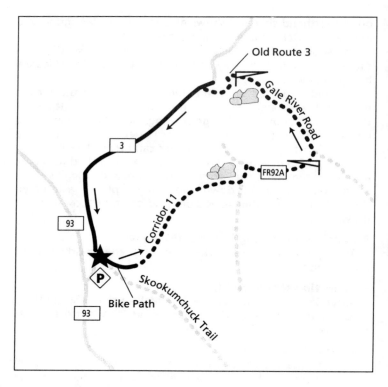

which looks down upon Route 3.

### 7.1 Route 3 (Make left)
Old Route 3 crosses Route 3 by two large boulders. Make a left here on Route 3 for an easy spin on a road with good shoulders.

### 10.0 Skookumchuck Trailhead (Make left)
At the 10 mile mark, make a left back to the trailhead where you started.

# 34. Stinson Lake Challenge

**INTERMEDIATE
28.5 MILES**

- ■ **WHERE IS IT?** Near Plymouth
- ■ **SURFACE:** Paved back roads (three mile dirt section)
- ■ **STARTING POINT:** Small parking area by Blair Covered Bridge.
- ■ **DIRECTIONS:** From I-93, exit 27, make left. At blinking yellow light, go straight to covered bridge.
- ■ **FOOD AND STUFF:** Plymouth has bike shops and food. Rumney and Stinson Lake has small stores.

Stinson Lake seems like a secret place. Situated in the hills of Rumney, the lake and little villages in the area take on a sleepy but serene flavor. Cycle on the shores of the lake and see smart, summer homes. Leave the picturesque shores and take in a bit more color and funk.

Though somewhat isolated on the southwest edge of the White Mountains, this nearly 30 mile loop is an incredible challenge. Massive hills await the cyclist after the oh-so-charming village of Rumney. Up into Ellsworth, where impressive mountain views appear through the trees, road riders will get a White Mountain workout.

It appears as this can't be so, as the ride begins in the gentle backroads of Campton and Plymouth where farms and fields rule the roost in the valley. As the elevation changes, so does the challenge. A long, arduous 5 mile climb takes riders to the lake. The climb doesn't end there. Past the shores, the climb continues, some of it on a dirt section. The descent is exhilarating, combining the winding road in Ellsworth with mountain scenery.

### 0.0 Start Blair Covered Bridge parking area

Leave the parking area by heading for the blinking traffic light and stop sign.

### .1 Junction with Route 3 (Make left)

Turn left on Route 3, heading for Plymouth. Ride along the banks of the Pemigewasset River and head into Plymouth after about 2.4 miles. The shoulder will vary along the commercial stretch.

### 3.3 Junction with Fairgrounds Road (Make right)

Turn right on Fairgrounds Road at about 3.3 The road rolls along in a pleasant mix of scenery.

### 6.5 Junction with Quincy Road (Make right)

Turn right on Quincy Road at about the 6.5 mark at a beautiful junction of field and farm. Roll on past the airport and the distant hills. At around 9.3 there is about a half mile climb, passing a few roadside boulders. Then dip on down and into Rumney.

### 10.8 Junction with Stinson Lake Road (Make right)

Turn right at the stop sign in Rumney at about 10.8. In the village, opportunity exists for re-fueling at the Rumney Village Store. Leaving Rumney village, the climbing begins right on past the historic Mary Baker Eddy historical house.

Near the 12 mile mark, a traffic sign with a swiggley arrow sets the tone for what the terrain will be like for the next 5 miles. Don't work so hard that you can't admire the stone walls and Stinson Brook along the way. Stinson Lake Road does provide some dips for occasional relief during the climb. Check out the self-proclaimed eye sore store at about the 15 mile mark. This is your signal that Stinson Lake is soon ahead. The Stinson Lake Store is situated at about 15.4.

Roll along the shore and drink in the views at the base of Stinson Mountain.

The road will turn to dirt at about the 16.8 mark in Ellsworth for about a 3 mile stint on hardpack. There is also a change in the name of the road. It is now Ellsworth Road. The road is very hilly. Enjoy the flowing waters at about 17.6 and the creative homes near the 18 mile mark. The terrain can be steep at times.

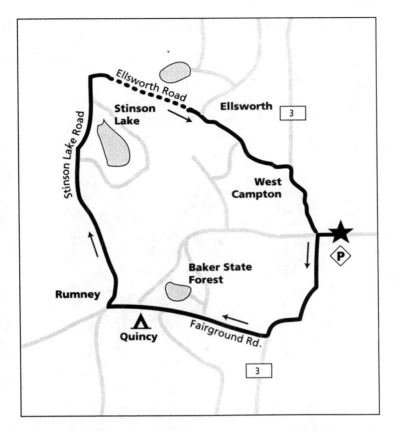

At around the 20.5 mark, a descent begins with grades of 15 percent. The road returns to pavement near the 20.6 mark. Get some speed as the road bottoms out by a church and starts up again into Campton.

Near 22.7, a sign indicates a long descent of 13 percent for some 2.75 miles. Check those brakes. Put on that smile. Look at those stunning mountains on the left.

### 25.4 Junction with Dan Web Road (Make left)

Turn left at the stop sign and head downhill.

### 25.5 Junction with Route 3 (Make right)

There's a second stop sign. Make a right here on Route 3 and head south. Those needing a rest might consider the Sunset Grill off to the left in the distance. Route 3 rolls a bit, with the shoulder varying along the way. Zip along the Pemi.

### 28.4 Junction with Blair Road (Make left)

Turn left at the blinking yellow light on Blair Road

### 28.5 Blair Covered Bridge parking area.

Nice job!

**INTERMEDIATE
14 MILES**

# 35. Sugar Hill Loop

- ■ WHERE IS IT? Franconia, Sugar Hill
- ■ SURFACE: Paved backroads
- ■ STARTING POINT: Parking area off Main Street in Franconia.
- ■ DIRECTIONS: Take exit 38 off I-93 and follow signs to Franconia's Main Street.
- ■ FOOD AND STUFF: It's right there in Franconia. There's a bike shop on Main Street.

The Franconia, Sugar Hill and Easton area is a gem in the Granite State. Life seems to take its time on the roads less traveled. Open fields and farms dot the landscape on the western side of the White Mountains. This is an area which gave inspiration to the poet Robert Frost. Here, in tiny Sugar Hill, is the site of the first ski school in North America. There is actually a road called Lover's Lane, quaint town buildings, inns, laidback stores and a fine gastronomical treat — Polly's Pancake Parlor. This is a ride with lots of sideshow potential. Either zip right through it, or slow down for the museums, inns and shops.

Though charming, Sugar Hill's name might set off some bells in a bicyclist's head. Yes, there are climbs. But the ride down from Sugar Hill back into Franconia will certainly end with a smile.

**0.0 Start on Main Street in Franconia, across from the Franconia Sports Shop.**
Head for the blinking yellow light.

### .1 Left on Route 116

Make a left on Route 116 south. Gaze up at the yellow Dow Academy building set against the mountains. Route 116 will roll up gently from the valley floor with the Kinsman Range smack ahead of you. The shoulder will quickly disappear, replaced by rushing waters along the roadside.

At about the 1 mile mark, the opportunity is unveiled to visit the Frost Place, Robert Frost's former home. To get there, make a right on Bickford Hill Road and go a quarter mile. There is a museum with Frost memorabilia and the delightful Poetry Trail, set among a mossy stone wall, wildflowers and birches.

Near the 2.3 mile mark, the handsome Franconia Inn is passed and soon, the Franconia Airport. It is possible to take a ride in those gliders and soar above the very area you are cycling. Look for the scarecrows as you cycle past farms. Actually, this is a working farm area, so get ready to wave if you see a farmer on a tractor pulling hay.

### 5.8 Sugar Hill Road (Make right)

Turn right on Sugar Hill Road and start to climb on the backcountry road laced with pleasant homes, gardens and views. There is some relief during the two mile uphill.

### 8.0 Junction with sign to Sugar Hill (Make right)

Turn right on Dyke Road and enjoy a quick, sharp descent. The road will sweep around to the left to Easton Road. Be sure you stay on Easton. After that zippy downhill, the road goes and up and down for another 2 miles, passing more farms, colorful fences, and stables.

### 10.2 Junction 117 east (make right)

Turn right on Route 117 east and pedal into Sugar Hill proper, dripping with New England quaintness. The white meetinghouse has an inviting bench. Send a postcard from the tiny post office. Stop in at the Sugar Hill Historic Museum with its displays of early pioneer mountain life and replica of a 19th century tavern kitchen. Well worth a stop is Harman's Cheese and Country Store with its aged gourmet treats for both the taste buds and olfactory organ.

Continue up on Route 117, passing the community church, a sign for Lover's Lane, and another inn. At about the 11.2 mark

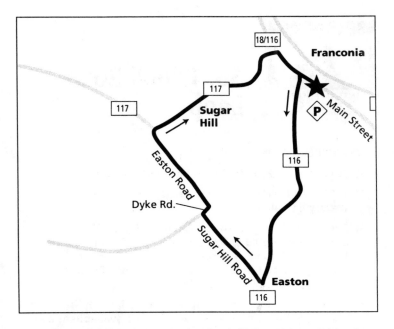

is the Sugar Hill Sampler, a spot for jellies and jams. This place actually made news when a New York City reporter stopped in to buy some gifts and could pay with a check. He actually wrote about it! That's enough climbing for this ride. Get ready to roll!

Before you pick up too much speed, consider stopping at Polly's Pancake Parlor at about the 12 mile mark. Choose from several types of pancakes, served in two waves.

The road declines sharply, with a sign indicated it is an eight percent grade. Enjoy!

### 13.5 Junction with 18/116 (Make right)

The exhilarating two mile downhill must end at the junction with Routes 18/116. Turn right here and you will be back on Main Street in Franconia, soon passing an ice cream shop and then bakery.

### 13.9 End

Back at the parking area.

**INTERMEDIATE
32 MILES**

# 36. Tripoli Road Loop

■ WHERE IS IT? Waterville Valley

■ SURFACE: Backroads, 5 mile hardpack section

■ STARTING POINT: Livermore Road trailhead in Waterville Valley.

■ DIRECTIONS: To get there, take exit 28 off I-93 and travel on Route 49 to Waterville Valley. Turn left onto Tripoli Road, then bear right at the "Y" after a mile. Turn right a half mile later on West Branch Road. The parking area is over the bridge.

■ FOOD AND STUFF: There's food and a bike shop in Waterville Valley's Town Square. Food is available at a few campgrounds along the way and at a general store in Campton.

The Tripoli Road Loop rolls through several small communities on the western side of the White Mountains. Though there is about 5 miles of hardpacked dirt on Tripoli Road, cyclists still use it as part of this nearly 32 mile ride. Now, this loop can be done in either direction. By riding it this way, the hardpack is ridden at the beginning, and soon forgotten for the bucolic Route 175 as it follows the Pemigewasset River before hooking up with Route 49, also a picturesque road leading to Waterville Valley.

Just a note that on summer weekends, Tripoli Road can be crowded. The road, closed from November until May, is maintained by the U.S. Forest Service and is called a roadside dispersed camping area. That means there aren't any developed

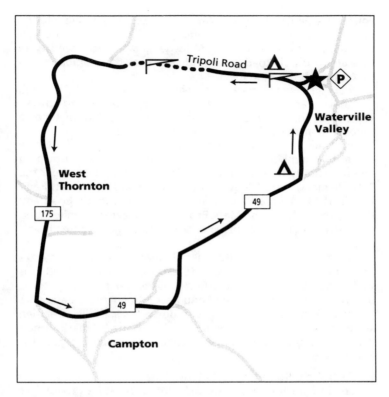

sites on the road, but established ones. There are no formal potable water sources, no fireplaces and no restroom facilities. Campers head into the woods and set up shop by an established site. It's a bit rustic and very popular.

### 0.0 Start Livermore Road Trailhead
Leave the Livermore Road trailhead, head over the bridge and ride out to Tripoli Road.

### .1 Tripoli Road (Make right)
Turn right on Tripoli Road and begin to ascend. This section of the road is paved. At .3 a gate is passed and a sign welcomes

you to the White Mountain National Forest. A half mile into the ride, pass the Osceola Vista Campground and snake up under the canopy of trees overhead. Mileage markers are placed every mile along Tripoli Road, giving riders a sense of accomplishment as it parallels the Mad River.

Near the 2.9 mile mark, the pavement turns to dirt. The road will have varying conditions, from hardpack dirt to gravel. Watch out for potholes and washboard sections from time to time. Also at this point is the Mt. Osceola trailhead.

The really good news is that it is time for a zipper of a 4 mile descent. A number of trailheads will be passed, some providing an opportunity for offshoot rides on a mountain bike. Near the 3.9 mile mark, Tripoli Road crosses Beaver Pond Road. East Pond Trail is at the 4.5 mark. Near 5.9 is the Hix Mountain Road and shortly thereafter is the Mack Brook Road. Near the 7 mile mark, the road sweeps up a bit, and drops down again after a half mile.

Pass a gate at around the 7.8 mile mark, and find a pay station. This is a place to get permits to camp off Tripoli Road. It is staffed during certain hours. Shortly thereafter, the road returns to pavement and the Russell Pond Recreation Area is passed.

Tripoli Road continues to sweep down for a 2 mile screamer, leave the National Forest and pass a gate at the 9.4 mark. Tripoli Road now has a shoulder and continues under an overpass for Interstate 93.

### 9.9 East Side Road/Route 175 (Make left)

Turn left on Route 175 south, one of the state's roads less taken. Sandwiched at times between the interstate and the more traveled Route 3, Route 175 toys with the Pemigewasset River in a cat and mouse game. It comes close to its banks, crosses it, runs along it and then shoots away into the woods. There are some spectacular views (particularly at the onset), stretches of solitude and a small town or two. The shoulder is narrow and will disintegrate.

At about 11.4, there is a private camping area.

### 11.6 Route 175 (Bear right)

Route 175 comes to a junction with Thornton Gore Road. The parking area is entrance to a hidden gorge, popular for swimming.

Turn right, cross the bridge and head up the hill where about a half mile you will pass a campground and enter the boundary of Thornton. The campgrounds are opportunities for food, if needed.

Roll and ramble along the quiet backroad for a few miles.

Near the 16 mile mark the town of Thornton, with its ball-field, cemetery and then a golf driving range come into view. A mile later, pass the library and school.

Campton is the next town to be entered at about the 19.6 mark. There's a general store, the Campton Cupboard, to refuel if needed.

### 20.1 Route 49 (Make left)

Turn left at the stoplight on Route 49, heading east. The turn onto Route 49 is open and scenic. There is a dam, rushing waters and just wonderful views. To add to the experience, there is a nice-sized shoulder. Route 49 runs along the Mad River and leads to the Waterville Valley ski area, rolling with mountain views and opportunities for hiking and camping. Signs along the way will indicate mileage to the ski area.

Shortly, it's back into the White Mountain National Forest and a forest campground. A restaurant is passed at the 22.4 mile mark and a mile later, the road to Sandwich Notch appears. Mad River Road is at 24.7 and a picnic area is at 25.8. At 29.3, there is the Sandwich Mountain Trailhead.

### 29.6 Tripoli Road (Make left)

An old friend returns. Make a left on Tripoli Road. There is the Waterville camping area and gas station with food here. Quickly, the road climbs for about a half mile, but then descends again.

### 30.9 Tripoli Road (Bear right)

The road forks, bear right on Tripoli Road. There is a sign saying the road is closed from November to May.

### 31.5 Livermore Road Trailhead (Make right)

Turn right into the Livermore Road trailhead, where the ride began.

**ADVANCED
17 MILES**

# 37. Tunnel Brook/ North South Loop

- ■ WHERE IS IT? Benton, near Lincoln and Franconia
- ■ Surface: Forest road, singletrack, doubletrack, pavement
- ■ STARTING POINT: Forest Road 7 in Benton.
- ■ DIRECTIONS: Head west from North Woodstock on Route 112 off Interstate-93 (Exit 32). Travel 11 miles, and make left on Tunnel Brook Road. The road turns to dirt at .7, and at 1.4 there is an intersection. Park at the small trailhead at Forest Road 7 on the left, just past the gate.
- ■ FOOD AND STUFF: Carry it with you! There is no water or food. Afterwards, try North Woodstock and Lincoln.

Mountain goats will want to head for this challenging White Mountain loop. Slackers dare not tread here. Though upper level intermediates will be able to tackle this ride, those cyclists who don't like to get off their bikes won't have much fun.

Why do this ride? There is a mixed bag of terrain. Some might be intimidating, while some might bring a smile. Yes, while descending a 2 mile section of singletrack from a troika of ponds on the Tunnel Brook Trail, it would be best to crack open a can of smiles and drink deeply.

There are technical sections and a punishing 3.5 mile climb up the North South Road right after the singletrack. North South is a sneaky road. The climb is gradual and there are several false summits. But, it's also about 3.5 miles down the other side.

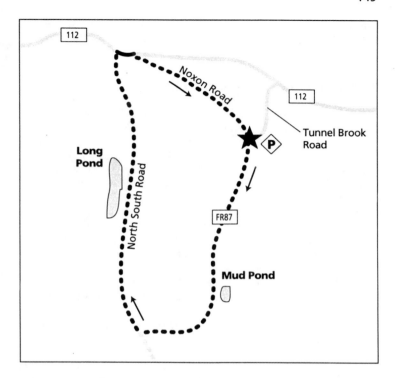

However, there isn't much civilization out this way. And chances are, you won't find many motorists out this way either.

The loop cuts between Mounts Moosilauke and Clough at the beginning while paralleling the Tunnel Brook. Along the way, enjoy the spendor of heading up to Mud Pond. Then, Jeffers Brook comes along for the ride up North South Road to vistas of Long Pond. There is also an option for a side trip up Blueberry Mountain and some exposed rock riding for the most advanced of cyclists.

## 0.0 Start at Forest Road 7

Begin by pedaling on Forest Road 7, a dirt road. The beginning of the ride starts with a gradual three-quarter of a mile climb before there is some relief. The road then rises again before letting gravity play. Pass the trailhead for the Benton Trail to Mount Moosilauke at about 1.5. Forest Road 7 dead-ends at about 2.3.

## 2.3 Tunnel Brook Trail (Go straight)

Pick up the well-marked Tunnel Brook Trail for about 4.4 miles. The trail begins as an old logging road. Be prepared for three stream crossings over the next quarter of a mile. Water bars are also obvious. It will start to get more technical. But there is also a nice section along the banks of Tunnell Brook.

At about 3 miles, the trail enters a grove with a nice rideable surface. But don't get complacent. Up ahead are some very rocky, wet and muddy sections where dismounting should be considered.

More stream crossings and a taste of singletrack comes up. Then, it's rocky again.

At about 3.5, off to the left is a spot to view the sides of Mount Clough. Cairns mark the trail.

At about 3.8, the trail comes to the first of three ponds. It is unrideable around this first one. So walk and get ready for a few stream crossings.

Near 4.2 on the left is a fire ring. There is a beaver dam there and views up Mount Moosilauke.

When you get to the blue painted rock at about 4.5, the fun soon begins. This is some of the nicest singletrack around. Enjoy the downhill as the trail heads along a ridge. Caution: there will be times to dismount for steep embankments and stream crossings on the descent near Slide Brook!

The trail passes a reservoir and shortly thereafter, an abandoned camp as it turns to doubletrack.

After the camp, the trail ends at the sign.

## 6.7 Intersection with North South Road (Make right)

Turn right and head up the North South Road for a long, slow climb. Ride gradually for 3.5 miles up the packed road as Jeffers Brook snakes along. There is an opportunity for a side trip at 7.1. On the left, the Blueberry Mountain Trailhead appears. The trail follows an old logging road and is for advanced riders. The appeal is the many open ledges. Turn back at around the 1.8

mile mark if you go.

The 9.3 mark is a seemingly false summit. The road really starts to roll down at about 10.3. Then, zip on down for about 3.5 miles, looking for the views of Long Pond on the left at about 10.8.

## 14.0 Intersection with Route 116 (Make right)

Turn right at the stop sign and follow Route 116. There won't be a sign. Pass some residences and a garage.

## 14.2 Intersection with Noxon Road (Make right)

The first right is Noxon Road. There is no sign. Make a right. Just a few more bursts up and then sweet downhills. This is the final leg, passing by a few homes in this quiet section of the White Mountains.

The road turns to dirt for stretch and then back to pavement. At about 16.3, it turns to dirt of the remainder of the journey. When it does, zip on down for about a mile and a smile.

## 17.1 Intersection with Forest Road 7 (Make right)

There's the car!

**EASY
7 MILES**

# 38. Wells Road Loop

■ WHERE IS IT? Franconia

■ SURFACE: Paved backroads

■ STARTING POINT: Parking area, Main Street, Franconia.

■ DIRECTIONS: Take exit 38 on I-93 to Main Street.

■ FOOD AND STUFF: Franconia has a bike shop and food. Inns dot this ride.

Short and scenic can best describe this easy spin through Franconia. Although the mileage is short, there is much to do along this backroad loop. Gaze upon the Kinsman Range. Have lunch at a country inn. Stop at a gift shop. Explore Robert Frost's mountain farm. Watch the gliders dance among the thermals. This is one of those gentle, relaxing rides for everyone and should be savored.

### 0.0 Start Main Street, Franconia

Parking can be found off Main Street across from the Franconia Sport Shop. This is where the ride begins. Go through the blinking yellow light, heading south on Route 18. Look at Cannon Mountain in the background. Keep an eye out for Our Lady of the Snows Church, town hall, the museum and information booth. Ramble through the pretty mountain town. Listen for the waters that parallel the road. Inns and restaurants dot the road. Pop into the Green Frog gift shop to see what finds you. There's a campground up ahead and then Lovett's Inn.

## 2.4 Wells Road (Make right)

The gentle, rolling road leads past the Horse and Hound Inn on the left. Be sure to look up at the mountain views. The road runs past a number of residences. At the 3.4 mile mark, do not bypass this incredible photo opportunity at Lake Densmore with the Kinsman Range in the background.

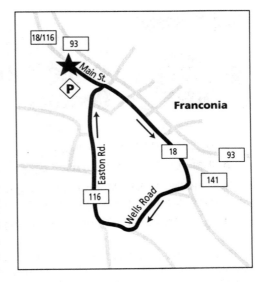

## 4.5 Easton Road (Route 116 north) (Make right)

After rolling through the woods, the ride opens up on the valley floor. Make a right. That's the Franconia Airport where gliders take off to ride the thermals. Pull over and watch them if there is activity. At about the 4.8 mile mark on the left is the Franconia Inn with its white clapboards and green shutters. The Frost Place is a fine diversion at the 6.1 mile mark. Make the left on Bickford Road if you care too, and pedal the quarter mile to the mountain farm of poet Robert Frost. There is a museum.

Soon, the village of Franconia comes into view with churches, school and bridge.

## 7.1 Main Street (Make left)

At the blinking yellow light, make a left on Main Street and head back to the parking lot.

**INTERMEDIATE
102 MILES**

# 39. White Mountain Triple Notch Century

- ■ WHERE IS IT? North Conway
- ■ SURFACE: Pavement (Road/bike paths/bike lanes)
- ■ STARTING POINT: Municipal parking lot, Main Street, North Conway, diagonally across from Schouler Park.
- ■ FOOD AND STUFF: There is a lot along the way.

The White Mountain Triple Notch Century circles right through the heart of the White Mountains. The spectacular scenery, fine roads, ample attractions and three mountain passes make 100 mile loop a goal for both the rider seeking the day century prize and the bicycle camper looking for a two or three day overnight adventure.

The three passes tackled during this ride are Kancamagus Pass, Franconia Notch and Crawford Notch. All three involve long climbs at times. However, the downhill rewards are worthwhile. During the century, riders will have ample opportunity for food, with the exception of about a 30 mile stretch on the Kancamagus Highway. Water is readily available.

The shoulder varies along the ride. The Kancamagus Highway has a narrow shoulder while the Connector Road from the Kancamagus is a bike route as is Route 3. The Franconia Notch Bike Path is for riders and walkers. Route 3 towards Twin Mountain varies in width as does Route 302 down through Crawford Notch.

Ample opportunity exists to break this ride down into an overnight. Campgrounds, inns and motels are scattered throughout the area.

This loop can be done in either direction.

## 0.0 Start Municipal parking area, Main Street, North Conway.

Exit the parking area by turning right onto Main Street.

## .4 Junction with River Road (Turn left)

At the traffic lights, turn left on River Road. Ride over the Saco River and soon admire the views of Mount Washington and the climbing ledges — White Horse and Cathedral — of North Conway.

## 1.4 Junction with West Side Road (Turn left)

Make a left at the junction with West Side Road and follow the bike lane which rolls past farms, farm stands, mountain views and covered bridges. There is a railroad crossing at about 5.6

The bike lane ends as West Side Road becomes Washington Street in Conway Village.

## 7.9 Junction with Route 16 (Turn right)

At the traffic lights, make a right on Route 16, heading south through Conway. If you haven't stocked up on food by now, this is almost the last chance to do it before Lincoln. About 8.4 is a railroad crossing.

## 8.7 Junction with Route 112 west, the Kanacamagus Highway (Turn right)

Turn right by the light on Route 112 west. This is the Kancamagus Highway. The "Kanc" is a Scenic Byway, achieved because of its recreational opportunities and aesthetic, cultural and historical values. It winds its way from the Saco to Pemigewasset Rivers, about 34 miles from Conway to Lincoln. The highest point is 2,855 feet above sea level.

There are a number of campgrounds, vistas and picnic tables along the Kancamagus.

Soon after turning onto the highway, a ranger information station appears on the right. Just up the road is Baldy's Diary Bar on the left. This is the last chance for food and drink before Lincoln. Ask if you can see the snowshoe museum.

The Kanc narrowly winds and rolls along. Let's break down a popular misconception: it is not all uphill this way. There is both up and down before the steep pull up to the pass. Until then, it is a very enjoyable ride with much to see.

Passaconaway Road is passed at about 15.1. A right here leads to a covered bridge, campground and toilets. Just on the left is another campground called Blackberry Crossing.

Lower Falls Scenic Area, at 15.8, is worth a peek to watch the water cascade over the huge rocks. Admire the ledges. You'll feel the incline on the road at this point.

The Rocky Gorge Scenic Area, where the Swift River has worn out the solid rock, is worth a stop too. That's at about 18 on the right.

Cycle down a few miles as you cross the junction with Bear Notch Road at about 21.3. The Jigger Johnson Campground and Passaconaway Historic Site is about 2 miles thereafter. The short walk to Sabbaday Falls is worth a diversion at about 24.6. There's a toilet there too.

Near the 26 mile mark, the road begins its 5 mile quest for the top of the pass. The road winds somewhat steeply at this point. The reward will be both an internal feeling of accomplishment and a thrilling downhill. Near the top is a scenic outlook and picnic tables.

After the top at about 31.4, strap on that seatbelt because it's time for 13 miles of mostly downhill, including "S" and hairpin turns. The grade is about nine percent at the beginning.

There are a number of camping and toilet facilities during the descent. At 36.6, the Otter Rocks Rest Area has toilets. One mile later is the Big Rock Campground. Near the 40 mile mark, the Lincoln Woods parking area is found. It has toilets too. Hancock Camping is at the 40.1 mark.

Leave the forest boundary and soon come upon Loon Mountain Park with its mountain biking facilities, scenic gondola rides and more at 42.3.

Enter Lincoln, where the shoulder widens and civilization in terms of food, ATM machines, bike shops and motels beckon.

## 44.6 Junction with Connector Road (Make right)

Turn right at the traffic lights onto Connector Road. It's a road with a wide shoulder that's a bike route.

## 45.7 Junction with Route 3 north (Make right)

Turn right at the stop sign onto Route 3. It also is a bike route

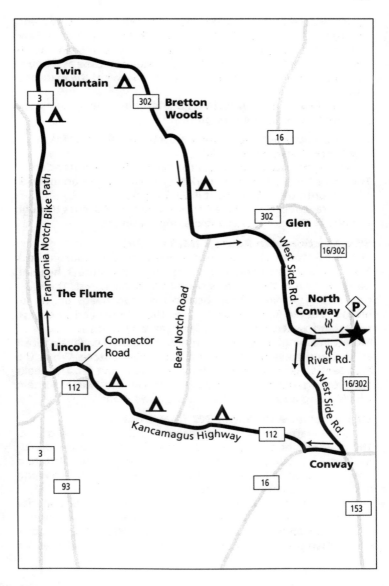

with a wide shoulder. During this next stretch you'll pass plenty of attractions (Clark's Trading Post, Whale's Tale Water Park, Indian Head Tower), motels, convenience stores and restaurants. The road switches from fairly level to a steady incline as it begins to climb up to Franconia Notch. Enjoy the views of the Franconia Range.

Enter Franconia Notch State Park at about the 49 mark and prepare to pick up the bike path.

### 49.2 Junction with Franconia Notch Bike Path. (Make right, then immediate left)

Turn right into the parking area for the Flume Visitor Center. There are toilets. Enter the parking area and make an immediate left onto the bike path. It is well-signed.

The Franconia Notch Bike Path stretches for 8.8 miles through the notch. Camping is available along its length.

### 58.0 Junction with Route 3 (Make right)

The bike path ends at the trailhead for the Skoocumchuck Trail. Leave the trailhead and make a right on Route 3, heading north. Return to the White Mountain National Forest. There is a nice rolling 4 mile section before the road heads up on an incline. Beaver Brook Rest Area at the 63.6 mark has toilets, tables and water. Rolling hills lead the way to distant views of Mount Washington, which then hide for a bit. Leave the forest at 65.5 and soon thereafter is a convenience store. When the Presidentials come into view, Twin Mountain isn't far. The peaks stand tall against the sky. Enjoy the descent into Twin Mountain which is also a spot for food and accomodations.

### 68.1 Junction with Route 302 (Make right)

At the traffic lights, turn right on Route 302, heading east. The road rolls at this point with a nice shoulder and commanding views. Coming up is a return into the White Mountain National Forest in about a mile and then a chance for camping at Zealand Recreation Area (70.3).

There is a convenience store at 72.5 that deserves a special note. They play classical music on the speakers outside which is quite a nice touch. Yes, classical gas. The Bretton Woods Sports Park is then on the right. It has mountain biking facilities and a scenic chairlift ride. After that at around 73 miles, there are train tracks to cross. A half mile later, keep your eyes peeled for a stunning vista of the Mount Washington Hotel against the Presidentials.

Roll on and get ready for Crawford Notch. There will be a short pull to the top of Crawford Notch where you will find the Appalachian Mountain Club hostel, information center, Saco Lake, toilets and stop on the Conway Scenic Railroad. Look for Elephant Head on the left, a rock formation before zipping down.

The ride down Crawford Notch is long and beautiful. It's about 14 miles of bicycle-friendly cruising, with the occasional push up, into Bartlett. In the notch, the rock formations ice over in the winter and are used by ice climbers. The train chugs through it. It also offers fine hiking trails, including having the Appalachian Trail cross it.

The steep and winding road (13 percent) begins its descent at about the 77 mile mark. You will be cycling through Crawford Notch State Park for about 6 miles. Pass the two waterfalls on the left — Flume Cascade and Silver Cascade.

The shoulder will eventually narrow a bit.

The Willey House and its inviting paths come into view at about the 79.6 mile mark. There's lots of history here about the Willey family and the rock slide that caused their deaths. There's a snack bar here. At 82.5, camping is available at the Dry River Campground. The 84 mile mark brings a campground and convenience store. Pass the Notchland Inn at around 85.3 and climb a short stretch. This is the tiny community of Hart's Location. How tiny is it? Town Hall is in the town clerk's home basement.

Fourth Iron is a campground on the left about 88 miles into the ride. Leave the forest just over a mile later. There's a final rest area with toilets and tables on the right. At 89.7, another general store is available.

Roll into Bartlett, first crossing the train tracks at about 91.4. Bartlett will have inns, motels and food.

The shoulder narrows through Bartlett. There will be another track crossing at about 93.8. The Attitash Bear Peak Ski Area, with its mountain biking, chairlifts, water slide and alpine slide is passed at about 94.3.

### 94.9 Junction with West Side Road (Make right)

Turn right on the shoulderless West Side Road and enjoy the final meandering leg of this journey. The road winds and rolls by the Saco River. Keep an eye on that odometer to watch it reach the big century.

When the road opens up by the strawberry fields, the end is near.

There is one final push up the hill after First Bridge.

### 101.6 Junction with Main Street (White Mountain Highway) (Make right)

Turn right at the lights on Main Street.

### 102.0 Municipal Parking (Make left)

Turn left into the parking area.

# 40. White Mountain Traverse

**ADVANCED
60 MILES**

- ■ WHERE IS IT? Jefferson to Sandwich
- ■ SURFACE: Forest road, logging road, doubletrack, singletrack, pavement
- ■ STARTING POINT: Jefferson Notch Road parking area
- ■ DIRECTIONS: From Route 2 in Jefferson, turn on Valley Road. Drive 1.25 miles and make a left on Jefferson Notch Road. Continue .7 miles to the parking area on the right.
- ■ FOOD AND STUFF: It's best to have everything you need. Water filters and purifcation tablets should be considered for this ride. The availability of food is limited and far between. There is opportunity for food in Crawford Notch, Waterville Valley and Sandwich.

The White Mountain Traverse is a point-to-point adventure spanning the entire region from north to south. The mixed bag of terrain, four mountain passes, grueling uphills, scintillating downhills and magnificent scenery make this ride a most challenging journey. It is only for the most advanced of riders and can also be tackled as an overnight. Skilled riders could take advantage of the long hours of daylight in summer and conquer this ride in one very long day. During the magical days of autumn, this is the one.

In about 60 miles from Jefferson to Sandwich, the route takes on Jefferson Notch Road, the highest public road in the state at 3,009 feet. From there, zip down through Crawford Notch (approx.1900 feet) and head over to the Kancamagus Highway via the gentle 4 mile incline of Sawyer River Road. Head up the Kancamagus for a short spell and pick up the brutal Livermore Trail which crests at 2,864 feet. Enjoy the winding ride down Livermore Road. Conquer the ever-challenging Sandwich Notch Road at a patriotic 1,776 feet and roll right into the quiet of Sandwich.

For the most part, the traverse is on rider-friendly terrain. The Livermore Trail, which links the Kancamagus Highway to Waterville Valley, is the exception. Though the singletrack at the beginning is most welcome, it is short-lived. The hiking trail, up a steep, deep, wooded gorge with huge mossy rocks, becomes a push, pull and carry for a couple of miles. Mossy rocks are slippery. Legs sink knee-deep in foul-smelling mud. Be forewarned: use extreme caution on this leg of the ride.

Camping can be found at the White Mountain National Forest's Waterville site in Waterville Valley, about 37 miles into the trip.

Since this is a point-to-point trip, two cars are needed to make this work. There is a parking area near the beginning of Jefferson Notch Road. In Sandwich, municipal parking is available next to town hall on Route 113.

## 0.0 Start Jefferson Notch Road

(Mileage from beginning of Jefferson Notch Road)

Jefferson Notch Road (FR 4) is a steep, winding dirt road for about 9 miles which passes through Mount Jefferson and the Dartmouth Range. Pavement makes an appearance near the several bridges. The climb is a long, arduous 5.5 miles. Begin and soon enter the White Mountain National Forest. There is a parking area on the right at .7 mark. The northern end of the road is paralleled by the South Branch of the Israel River while the southern end runs along Jefferson Brook.

At 5.5, the trailhead for the Caps Ridge Trail is reached. This is the highest trailhead on a public road through the White Mountains. Head over to the sign. Take a picture. For those looking to start the day on a downhill note, begin the journey here and dispense with the long climb. From here, head on down for about 3.5 miles.

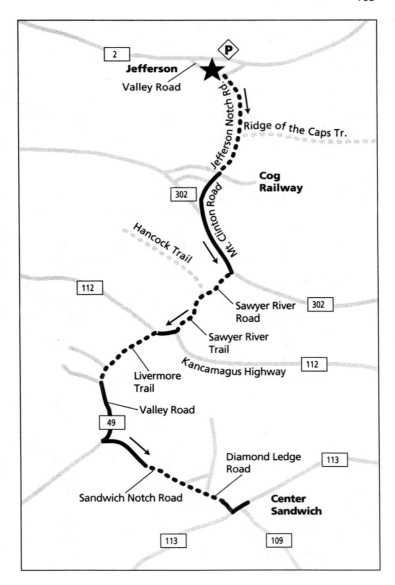

### 9.0 Junction with Mount Clinton Road (Go straight)

At about the 9 mile mark, Jefferson Notch Road ends at a junction with Base Road. Go straight to pick up the paved, rolling Mount Clinton Road.

### 12.5 Junction with Route 302 (Make left)

Turn left at about 12.5 on Route 302 and head east. The top of Crawford Notch has a lot of activity. There is the Appalachian Mountain Club's hostel, an information center, Saco Lake (the source of the river), Elephant Head Rock and a stop on the Conway Scenic Railroad.

Two waterfalls wait on the other side of the notch, but you will probably be going too fast to want to stop. Ride mostly downhill for several miles, passing the historic Willey House site (with snacks) at about the 15 mile mark. Near the 20 mile mark is a store for re-fueling.

### 23.5 Junction with Sawyer River Road (Make right)

Turn right at 23.5 on Sawyer River Road, an old logging road through deserted Livermore which is now never more. The road continues on a gentle 4 mile incline along the rushing Sawyer River. There is a footbridge over the river by the trailhead for the Sawyer Pond Trail at about 27.5. Continue straight on the Sawyer River Trail.

The road continues to climb just a bit more before rolling down to a junction.

### 28.8 Junction with Sawyer River Trail (Make left)

Turn left on the Sawyer River Trail at about 28.8. This is a well-signed intersection with the Hancock Notch Trail. Sawyer River Trail offers some fine singletrack. However, there are a number of bridge crossings during the ride, including a handful in the first three-tenths of a mile. The trail is mostly level, but there are some muddy and rooty sections. At about 30.8, there is a sign pointing to Bear Notch Road, Church Pond and the Nanamacomuck. Just stay straight on the Sawyer River Trail. Just after the 31 mile mark, there is a river crossing.

### 31.4 Junction with Kancamagus Highway (Make right)

The Sawyer River Trail ends at the Kancamagus Highway. Make a right at about 31.4 and head west on the Kancagamus

Climb up on the paved road for less than a mile to the trailhead with the Livermore Trail on the left.

## 32.2 Junction with Livermore Trail (Make left)

At about 32.2, make a left on the Livermore Trail. For nearly the next 8 miles, the combination of the Livermore Trail and Livermore Road will be the path to Waterville Valley. Livermore Trail is a hiking trail which starts out with promising singletrack in grassy clearings with pleasant views. About .6 mile into the trail, the path bears sharply to the left and enters into the woods. The trail becomes more rugged here, descending past a dry river bed. It becomes technical as it starts its climb up to Livermore Pass. Nearly 2 miles into the trail (34.2 on the ride) the unrideable section begins in earnest. The route heads up a deep gorge with big mossy, boulders. Though it will flatten up through Livermore Pass, the rocks persist, and so does mud. Once you reach a small waterfall with a sign indicating you have just traveled a mile since Livermore Pass, nirvana will soon return. There will be short bursts of singletrack followed by a nearly 5 mile descent down Livermore Road. Stay on Livermore Road, an access road for hikers, all the way down to the gate. When you see a wooden bridge on the left, bear to the right to stay on Livermore Road. Just a reminder that Livermore Road is popular with hikers, joggers and walkers. Be courteous even though you have just waded through the abyss between purgatory and hell.

Livermore Road ends at a gate. Go around the gate, cross the bridge and stop at the stop sign.

## 40.2 Junction with Tripoli Road (Make left)

Turn left on Tripoli Road.

## 40.8 Stop sign (Bear left)

Continue on Tripoli Road by making a left by the stop sign. Descend and soon you'll see a store on the left followed by a campground, Waterville, on the right. The campground is a good spot to spend the night. For those spending the night, a left on Valley Road gets you to Town Square in Waterville Valley.

## 42.6 Junction with Route 49/Valley Road (Make right)

Turn right onto Route 49 and head west. There are a couple

of picnic areas along the way. The ride descends along the Mad River.

### 48.8 Junction with Sandwich Notch Road (Make left)

Turn left on Sandwich Notch Road and begin the first of many steep climbs. The 8 mile rough road flirts between dirt and pavement. Cut in 1801, the road enabled farmers in northern New Hampshire and Vermont to get their produce to markets.

The road becomes narrow and winding. It has several blind spots. There are a few respites from the hard climbs and the views are outstanding as the area was a former farming region now almost completed reverted to forest. This is one of those roads that just keeps coming at you.

One such view is about a mile into the road with vistas of the Sandwich Range and backside of Waterville Valley. Head back into the woods for more climbing. The height of land is reached at about the 51.5 mark at 1,776. Don't rejoice too much, there is still more climbing. When the downhill comes, enjoy it for about 3 miles. There will be a few one lane wooden bridges to cross over, and the road will pass a number of trailheads (Algonquin, Guinea Pond, Sandwich Notch Park).

### 57.0 Junction with Diamond Ledge Road (Make right)

Bear right at Diamond Ledge Road as Sandwich Notch Road ends. Head up the hill, and in about .1, continue to bear right on Diamond Ledge Road. The road soon returns to pavement and when it does, get ready for a nice downhill. This is backroad New England at its finest. Admire the stone walls, handsome homes, farms and vistas.

### 59.0 Junction with Mount Israel Road (Bear right)

Continue on Diamond Ledge Road by bearing right as it intersects with Mount Israel Road.

### 59.4 Junction with Main Street (Make left)

At the stop sign on Main Street in Center Sandwich, make a left on Main Street. There is a store to the right if you need it.

### 59.6 Junction with Route 113 (Make left)

Turn left on Route 113 east, and cycle .1 to the municipal parking area on the left. Congratulations!

## SKI AREAS

It's time to head downhill.

Whether you're interested in screaming down slopes over waterbars on a full-suspension bike, maneuvering around rocks and stumps on singletrack or meandering along an old logging road, you'll find a sampling of terrain at the White Mountain ski areas offering mountain biking.

Many hardcore riders are attracted to the thrills and spills of downhill mountain biking. It isn't for everyone. White Mountain ski areas are trying to attract the more recreational rider by opening up trails that don't require lifts too. Several alpine areas offer lift-service mountain biking. Mountain bikers don't have to ride the lifts either. Many areas, both alpine and cross-country, offer passes to their Nordic networks.

But seriously, why pay for a trail pass if you can ride on the scores of trails in the area for free? The areas provide an element of safety. The trails are patrolled. They also give the illusion of wilderness to those unfamiliar with the woods and mountains. Though the trails are ridden, it's still only a mile or so to the payphone, restaurant and bike shop.

The ski areas also serve as the venue for races and fat tire events. Several offer shuttle services, guides, clinics, rental shops and tours as well. Most are open from late May to mid-October, but some offer just weekend hours of operation during the early and late parts of the season. It's always best to call ahead. Unless noted, phone numbers are with New Hampshire's 603 area code.

- **Attitash Bear Peak**
  Route 302, Bartlett; phone: 374-2368
  e-mail: info@attitash.com
  Internet: www.attitash.com

  *Lift-service is available. There are also several miles of gentle family terrain along the Saco River.*

- **The Balsams Wilderness**
  Route 26, Dixville Notch; phone: 800-255-0600
  e-mail: TheBALSAMS@aol.com
  Internet: www.thebalsams.com

  *Though north of the White Mountains, The Balsams Mountain Bike Center has about 35 miles of well-marked trails on its' cross-country network.*

- **Black Mountain**
  Route 16B, Jackson; phone: 383-4490
  e-mail: ski@blackmt.com
  Internet: www.blackmt.com.

  *Black Mountain does not open its' lifts to bikers in summer. However, they host a number of races.*

- **Bretton Woods**
  Route 302, Bretton Woods; phone: 800-232-2972;
  e-mail: skibw@brettonwoods.com
  Internet: www.brettonwoods.com.

  *Bretton Woods utilizes its' 60 miles of cross-country ski trails for mountain biking.*

- **Cannon Mountain**
  Franconia Notch State Parkway, Franconia
  Phone: 823-5563
  e-mail: cannon@connriver.net
  Internet: www.visitnh.gov.

  *Cannon does not offer lift service but there is a rental shop which suits those using the bike path through Franconia Notch.*

- **Franconia Village Cross-Country**
  Route 116, Franconia; phone: 800-473-5299
  e-mail: info@franconiainn.com
  Internet: www.franconiainn.com

  *About 40 miles of cross-country country ski trails are available to mountain bikers.*

- **Great Glen Trails**
  Route 16, Pinkham Notch; phone: 466-2333
  e-mail: greatgln@mt-washington.com
  Internet: www.mt-washington.com.

  *Great Glen's Nordic network is open to mountain bikers. They have a number of events and clinics.*

- **King Pine Ski Area**
  Route 153, East Madison; phone: 367-8896
  e-mail: purity@moose.ncia.net
  Internet: www.visitnh.gov.

  *Ten miles of cross-country ski trails are available for mountain biking to guests of Purity Spring Resort.*

- **Loon Mountain**
  Route 112, Lincoln; phone: 745-8111
  e-mail: info@loonmtn.com
  Internet: www.loon.com.

  *There's everything here from lift-service to 20 miles of cross-country trails to ride at Loon Mountain Park. Loon offers a shuttle service to the Franconia Notch Bike Path.*

- **Waterville Valley**
  Route 49, Waterville Valley; phone: 236-8311
  e-mail: info@waterville.com
  Internet: www.waterville.com.

  *The Snow's Mountain chairlift takes riders up to the summit while others like to explore the 30 miles of patrolled trails from Base Camp in Town Square.*

- **Phillips Brook Backcountry Recreation Area**
  PO Box 1076, Conway
  Phone: 447-1786, 1-800-TRAILS8
  e-mail: waltenburg@aol.com

  Though not a ski area, Phillips Brook is a unique backcountry experience with 100 miles of trails.

## BIKE SHOPS

Bike shops are your friends. Some even offer rentals. Treat employees with respect and they might share a few choice rides.

- **Bayside Bikes**
  4 Riverside Drive, Ashland
  Phone: 968-9676.

- **The Bike Shop**
  Mountain Valley Mall
  Boulevard, North Conway
  Phone: 356-6089

- **Boarder Town**
  Route 302, Glen
  Phone: 383-8981

- **Franconia Sport Shop**
  Main Street, Franconia
  Phone: 823-5241

- **Greasey Wheel**
  40 Main Street, Plymouth
  Phone: 536-3655

- **Joe Jones Ski and Sports**
  2709 Main Street,
  North Conway
  Phone: 356-9411

- **Joe Jones Ski and Sports**
  Route 49, Campton
  Phone: 726-3000

- **Littleton Bike Shoppe**
  87 Main Street, Littleton
  Phone: 444-3437

- **Moriah Sports**
  101 Main Street, Gorham
  Phone: 466-5050

- **Northern Extremes**
  Route 302, Glen
  Phone: 383-8117

- **Red Jersey Cyclery**
  Route 302, Glen
  Phone: 383-4660

- **Rhino Bike Works**
  95 Main Street, Plymouth
  Phone: 536-3919

- **Ski and Bike Warehouse**
  Main Street, Lincoln
  Phone: 745-3164

- **Ski Fanatics**
  Route 49, Campton
  Phone: 726-4327

- **Ski Works**
  Route 16,
  West Ossipee
  Phone: 539-2246

- **Sports Outlet**
  Main Street,
  North Conway
  Phone: 356-3133

- **White Mountain Cyclist**
  Main Street, Lincoln
  Phone: 745-8852

- **Ziel Schuss**
  24 Glen Road, Gorham
  Phone: 466-5756

## ORGANIZATIONS AND CLUBS

The following organizations and clubs are valuable resources for planning rides and trips in the White Mountains.

- **Appalachian Mountain Club**
  PO Box 298, Gorham, NH 03581
  Phone: 466-2721

- **White Mountain National Forest Headquarters**
  719 Main Street, Laconia, NH 03236
  Phone: 528-8721

- **Ammonoosuc Ranger Station**
  Box 239, Trudeau Road, Bethlehem, NH 03574
  Phone: 869-2626

- **Androscoggin Ranger Station**
  300 Glen Road, Gorham, NH 03581
  Phone: 466-2713

- **Evans Notch Ranger Station**
  18 Mayville Road, Bethel, Maine 04217
  Phone: 207-824-2134

- **Pemigewasset Ranger Station**
  RFD#3, Box 15, Route 175, Plymouth, NH 03264
  Phone: 536-1310

- **Saco Ranger Station**
  33 Kancamagus Highway, Conway, NH 03818
  Phone: 447-5448

- **New Hampshire State Parks**
  PO Box 1856, Concord, NH 03301
  Phone: 271-3556

- **New Hampshire Office of Travel
  and Tourism Development**
  Box 1856, Concord, NH 03302
  Phone: 271-2343 or 800-386-4664

- **Ski New Hampshire**
  PO Box 10, North Woodstock, NH 03262
  Phone 745-3002 or 800-887-5464

- **White Mountain Wheel People**
  c/o Red Jersey Cyclery
  PO Box 1209, Glen, NH 03838
  Phone: 383-4660

- **Granite State Wheelmen**
  2 Townsend Avenue, Salem, NH 03079
  Phone: 898-9926

- **Mount Washington Valley
  Chamber of Commerce**
  PO Box 2300, North Conway, NH 03860
  Phone: 356-3171 or 800-367-3364

- **Lincoln-Woodstock Chamber of Commerce**
  Box 358, Lincoln, NH 03251
  Phone: 745-6621 or 800-227-4191

- **International Mountain Bicycling Association**
  Box 7578, Boulder, CO 80306
  Phone: 303-545-9011

*Many maps and books about the White Mountains have been published. I've learned a great deal from them.*

## MAPS

- Mountain Bike Map of the Mount Washington Valley, MicroMap Graphics, 1996.

- Mountain Biking in the Northern White Mountains, Venture Project, 1991.

- The New Hampshire Atlas and Gazetteer, DeLorme Maps, 1996.

- White Mountain National Forest Mountain Bike Map: Pemigewasset Ranger District, U.S. Department of Agriculture, 1992.

## BOOKS

- Appalachian Mountain Club, AMC White Mountain Guide, 25th edition. Boston: Appalachian Mountain Club, 1992.

- Bernotas, Adolphe and Heavey, Tom and Susan, 30 Bicycle Tours in New Hampshire, 3rd. edition. Woodstock, VT: Backcountry, 1991.

- Johnstone, Stuart, Mountain Biking New Hampshire. Carlisle, MA: Active Publications, 1993.

*Also by Marty Basch*

# Against the Wind

**"Great fun to read."** — *Fairbanks, Alaska News Miner*

*In 1994, Basch rode from Maine to Alaska. Against the Wind is a collection of light-hearted tales of adventure. Meet a woman being carried to Alaska in a bicyclists' pannier. Ride along with a few down-and-out cyclists in British Columbia. Find out how the Royal Canadian Mounted Police tracked down the author's helmet. If you came face-to-face with a grizzly bear, what would you do? (ISBN 0-9646510-0-9, $12.95)*

# Above the Circle

**"...good summer read."** — *The Boston Globe*

Cycle among the reindeer near the top of the world. In 1996, Basch set out to ride near and above the Arctic Circle in Iceland, Norway, Sweden and Finland. Along the way he met Iceland's "tent man," a former Olympian with a most unusual lifestyle. While in Norway, Basch shared meals and stories with sled dog drivers who had raced in Alaska's Iditarod. Finland found him waking up to the Arctic Canoe Race while in Sweden, the "craziest cop in Sweden" entertained him with incredible tales.
(ISBN 0-9646510-1-7, $14.95)

Both books are available directly from
Top of the World Communications, PO Box 731,
Intervale, NH 03845. Please include postage and handling. Visit the Top of the World web site at www.mountwashingtonvalley.com/top-of-the-world or send e-mail to rodeman@aol.com.